T0375531

IN HIS NAME

A 30-DAY JOURNEY THROUGH THE NAMES OF GOD

JAMES JOHANNES

WESTBOW
PRESS®
A DIVISION OF THOMAS NELSON
& ZONDERVAN

WestBow Press books may be ordered through booksellers or by contacting:

WestBow Press
A Division of Thomas Nelson & Zondervan
1663 Liberty Drive
Bloomington, IN 47403
www.westbowpress.com
844-714-3454

ISBN: 979-8-3850-1711-9 (sc)
ISBN: 979-8-3850-1712-6 (hc)
ISBN: 979-8-3850-1713-3 (e)

Library of Congress Control Number: 2024901161

Print information available on the last page.

WestBow Press rev. date: 04/29/2024

CONTENTS

ACKNOWLEDGMENTS

With heartfelt gratitude and immeasurable love, I extend special thanks to my dear dad and mom. Your unwavering faith, your endless love, and your steadfast commitment to teaching me the ways of God from my earliest days have shaped my journey and kindled the flame of devotion within my heart. You are my earthly examples of His grace, and for that, I am eternally grateful.

Dear cherished reader,

May the pages that follow guide you closer to the heart of our Heavenly Father as we traverse the sacred landscape of His many names. Each name is a reflection of a facet of God's infinite character, a glimpse into His boundless love, grace, and power. May your journey through these pages deepen your connection, amplify your faith, and ignite a passion to know Him more intimately.

In every name, may you find solace, strength, and an invitation to draw nearer to the One who knows you by name and calls you His own.

With prayers and blessings,
James Johannes

INTRODUCTION

In the tapestry of human language, names hold a power that transcends the mere combination of letters and sounds. A name can tell a story, provide insight into character, and forge a connection that is both intimate and profound. In the sacred texts of the Bible, names are not only a means of identification but a window into the divine character of God. Each name attributed to the Almighty reflects a facet of His infinite complexity, offering us a glimpse into His nature, intentions, and unfathomable love for creation.

In His Name: A Thirty-Day Journey through the Names of God is an invitation to embark on a spiritual expedition to encounter the divine through the lens of His many names. Each day, we will pause to reflect on a different biblical name of God, seeking to understand more deeply who He is and how He works in our lives. This daily devotional is designed not just to inform but to transform, leading you into a richer, more vibrant relationship with the Creator.

Through the pages of this book, you will be guided step-by-step to

1. *discover a title*—a name of God that reveals a unique aspect of His character, each a stepping stone into deeper spiritual truths;
2. *explore scripture references*—to root your journey in the authoritative Word of God, anchoring each name in its scriptural context;
3. *delve into background context*—where we will unearth the historical and cultural significances behind the names, appreciating how they resonated with the people who first heard them;

4. *reflect with devotional content*—crafted to inspire, challenge, and encourage you in your daily walk, drawing practical insights from ancient truths;

5. *engage in prayer*—through crafted words that invite you to incorporate the day's name of God into your personal conversation with Him, deepening your relationship and dependence on Him; and

6. *apply action items and key takeaways*—practical steps and memorable truths to carry with you throughout your day, allowing the day's reflections to take root and grow in your life.

Each name of God is a thread in the greater narrative of the scripture, and as we explore these divine titles, we weave these threads into the fabric of our own stories. This journey is for the seeker of wisdom, the one who longs for a closer walk with God, and anyone who desires to understand the Almighty, not just by what He does but by who He is.

As you turn these pages and immerse yourself in the contemplation of God's names, may you find more than knowledge. May you encounter the living God. In His name, may your faith be strengthened, your hope renewed, and your love deepened.

DAY 1

ELOHIM: THE CREATOR GOD

> In the beginning, God created the heavens and the earth.
>
> —*Genesis 1:1 (NIV)*

Many people struggle with understanding the nature of God, often feeling overwhelmed by His complexity or even intimidated by His power, but that doesn't have to be the case. When we open our Bibles to Genesis 1:1, we are introduced to the name of God, which sets the stage for our understanding of His nature. The Hebrew word here is *Elohim (eh-loh-heem)*, which means *strong one* or *creator.* This word implies that God is not just powerful, but also creative and innovative. He didn't just make something out of nothing; He formed it with purpose and intent.

Elohim is our Creator, who has intricately designed every detail of this universe with absolute precision and love. Every mountain peak, grain of sand on the seashore, star in the sky, and cell in your body reflects His magnificent craftsmanship.

He did not create out of necessity or obligation but out of pure love and desire for a relationship. You are not an accident or a random occurrence; you were thoughtfully planned and lovingly crafted by Elohim Himself.

The beauty of Elohim is that this Creator doesn't stop at creation. In fact, His creativity is ongoing. As an artist continues to paint even after completing a masterpiece, so does Elohim continue to create in our lives today. He isn't done with us yet; there's more for Him to do in us and through us.

Elohim, the Creator God, made everything with purpose and intentionality, including you.

As we further explore Genesis 1:2 (NIV), we find that "the earth was formless and empty … and the Spirit of God was hovering over the waters." Even when things seem chaotic or without form like they did at creation's dawn, Elohim hovers over it all. He takes what appears meaningless or disordered and shapes it into something beautiful. With Elohim, emptiness is never the end of the story. Into the void, He speaks life, form, and order.

In times when life feels formless or void like an abyss—when you're facing confusion or uncertainty—remember that just as Elohim hovered over the face of those dark waters at creation's dawn, so too does He hover over your circumstances now. You may not see it immediately, but trust in His timing because He's shaping something beautiful from your chaos.

Even in chaos or disorder, Elohim creates order and beauty.

As we delve further into understanding Elohim as our Creator, we must realize that His creativity didn't cease after those six days mentioned in Genesis. He continues to create within us new hearts, spirits, and beginnings daily.

We often limit God's creative power to physical creation alone, when, in fact, He is continuously at work within us, shaping us more into His likeness each day. This process may be painful sometimes, but remember it's because He loves you too much to leave you as you are.

However, it's not always easy to understand or accept God's creative work in our lives. Sometimes we might feel like unfinished projects—flawed and incomplete. Remember, just as an artist takes time to perfect his masterpiece, so does Elohim take time to shape and mold us into His image.

> Trust in the LORD with all your heart; do not depend
> on your own understanding. (Proverbs 3:5 NLT)

To fully embrace Elohim's love for us means surrendering our need for control. We must trust in His plan even when we don't understand it. This requires humility and faith but brings peace beyond comprehension.

> Then God saw everything that He had made, and
> indeed it was very good. So the evening and morning
> were the sixth day. (Genesis 1:31 NKJV)

As you go about your daily life, remember to keep these truths at the forefront of your mind. Remember that Elohim created everything with purpose and intentionality—even you—and even when things seem chaotic or uncertain, He is still working to create something beautiful.

PRAYER:

Elohim, Creator God, I stand in awe of Your wondrous works. From the vastness of galaxies to the minute details of a single leaf, Your creativity knows no bounds. Help me to recognize Your hand in everything and to trust in Your power to bring order and beauty to my life. May I find rest in Your gentle presence, knowing You are always nearby. Amen.

Today, as you move through the hours, remember the majesty of Elohim, the Creator God. And let that inspire faith, wonder, and a deeper relationship with the One who crafted the universe and you.

ACTION STEPS:

1. Meditate on Genesis 1:1–2.
2. Whenever chaos seems overwhelming, remind yourself that Elohim creates beauty from chaos.
3. Write down areas where you've seen God's creative work in your life.
4. Pray, asking God to reveal His purpose for your creation.

IMPORTANT TAKEAWAYS:

- You were intentionally created by Elohim, the Creator God; this means you have inherent value and worth.
- Elohim continues His act of creation daily within us, constantly shaping us into His likeness.
- Understanding that we're created with a purpose can bring meaningfulness to our lives.
- Despite feeling unfinished at times, trust that God is still working on you because He sees the finished masterpiece even when we don't.

DAY 2

YAHWEH: I AM WHO I AM

> God said to Moses, "I AM WHO I AM." This is
> what you are to say to the Israelites: "I AM has sent
> me to you."
>
> —*Exodus 3:14 (NIV)*

The name *Yahweh (yah-way)*, translated as I AM WHO I AM, is a powerful reminder of God's eternal nature and unchanging character. In Exodus 3:14, when Moses asked God what he should tell the Israelites when they asked who sent him, God replied, "I AM WHO I AM." This profound statement is a name and a declaration of His being. It's akin to saying that He is the essence of existence itself.

To understand this better, let's consider the ocean. It's large and seemingly endless. You can't control it or contain it. Similarly, God is boundless in His power and presence. He exists beyond our comprehension and control. Yet like the ocean that provides life-sustaining water to our planet, God is also the source of all life.

God's self-identification as *I am* signifies His eternal existence. Unlike humans, who have a beginning and an end, God has always been and will always be. This concept may be difficult to grasp because everything we know in our physical world has a start and finish point. But remember, God operates outside these constraints.

When Moses asked for His name at the burning bush, God responded with "I AM WHO I AM," not as a casual response but as an affirmation of His absolute being. It wasn't about what He does or doesn't do but about who He is—eternal, omnipotent, and sovereign.

God remains consistent in a world where everything is subject to change and decay. He is the same yesterday, today, and forever.

The name Yahweh embodies the eternal and unchanging nature of God.

In today's society, where change seems to be the only constant thing, not knowing what tomorrow holds can be unsettling, but here lies your comfort; in an ever-changing world, you serve an unchanging God!

Understanding that *I am* implies present tense gives us comfort in knowing that God isn't just a historical figure or future hope—He's actively present in our lives right now every moment of every day, through joy and sorrow alike.

The implications of this are immense for your daily life! When you feel lost or uncertain about your future, remember that you are held by an eternal God who does not change with time or circumstances.

This knowledge should inspire confidence in your walk with Him. Just as He was faithful to Moses and the Israelites thousands of years ago, He remains faithful today because His character doesn't change.

> Jesus Christ is the same yesterday, today, and forever.
> (Hebrews 13:8 NLT)

Knowing Yahweh means acknowledging His active presence in our daily lives.

In our daily lives filled with uncertainty and change, it's easy to feel lost or overwhelmed. We may question our purpose or worth, but remembering Exodus 3:14 can provide comfort in these times—because God remains the same no matter what we're going through or how much we doubt ourselves or our circumstances.

"I am who I am" isn't merely a name; it's an invitation into a deeper relationship with our Creator. As we meditate on this profound truth and embrace its implications fully in our lives, we begin to experience peace that surpasses understanding.

FIVE FACETS UNCOVERED BY UNDERSTANDING YAHWEH:

1. *Eternal existence.* Our human minds struggle to comprehend eternity because everything around us has a beginning and an end. It is not so with Yahweh! He existed before time began and will continue to exist after time ceases.

   > "I am the Alpha and the Omega—the beginning and the end," says the Lord God. "I am the one who is, who always was, and who is still to come—the Almighty One." (Revelation 1:8 NLT)

2. *Unchanging nature.* The world around us is constantly in flux, but Yahweh stays unchanging. His love for us never wavers, His promises are steadfast, and His justice is unwavering.

3. *Promise of presence.* God's promise to Moses wasn't just for him; it extends to all believers today. No matter what we're going through, Yahweh promises to be with us every step of the way.

4. *Self-sustaining.* Unlike created beings who need external sustenance, Yahweh is self-sustaining. He doesn't need anything or anyone to exist or operate.

5. *Whole.* Understanding Yahweh means recognizing that God isn't one-dimensional but embodies all aspects of divinity—love, mercy, power, wisdom, etc., in perfect balance.

If you struggle with grasping these truths about Yahweh because of past experiences or misconceptions about Him, don't despair! Be patient with yourself as you allow these truths to sink deep into your heart over time through prayerful meditation on scriptures revealing His character.

PRAYER:

Dear Heavenly Father, thank You for revealing Yourself as the great I AM. Help me to trust in Your unchanging nature, especially when the world around me is in turmoil. May I always remember that You are self-existent, unchanging, and deeply personal. Draw me closer to You each day, and let my life reflect Your steadfast love and faithfulness. In Jesus's name, I pray. Amen.

As you move through your day, consider the areas in your life where you need to trust in the unchanging nature of God. Whether you're facing challenges, awaiting answers to prayers, or seeking direction, remember that God is the same steadfast I AM who appeared to Moses.

ACTION STEPS:

1. Spend time meditating on Exodus 3:14.
2. Write down any thoughts or insights that come to mind.
3. Pray for a deeper understanding of God's eternal nature.
4. Share these insights with a trusted friend or mentor.

IMPORTANT TAKEAWAYS:

- Yahweh means I AM WHO I AM, signifying God's eternal existence.
- God is vast, powerful, and beyond our control like an ocean.
- In an ever-changing world, we serve an unchanging God.

ᕷ Understanding God as I AM can bring peace and contentment to our lives.

ᕷ Our relationship with Him helps us grasp His eternal nature better.

DAY 3

EL SHADDAI: GOD ALMIGHTY

> When Abram was ninety-nine years old, the LORD
> appeared to him and said, "I am God Almighty; walk
> before me and be blameless."
>
> —*Genesis 17:1 (NIV)*

Dawn breaks and as you start your day, a profound message from the ancient scriptures waits to nourish your soul. Today we turn our hearts to a name of God that encapsulates His might and sufficiency: *El Shaddai (el shad-dye).*

The name El Shaddai is one of the many names given to God in the Bible. It's a Hebrew term that translates to God Almighty. This powerful declaration sets the tone for our understanding of who God is in our lives.

El Shaddai signifies a God who is all-sufficient and all-bountiful, the source of all blessings. He is not just a mighty God but the Almighty God. He can fulfill every promise He has made and answer every prayer we lift up. Remember this when you feel overwhelmed or uncertain, your problems are never bigger than El Shaddai.

Embrace the truth that El Shaddai is greater than any challenge you face.

As we look closer into understanding El Shaddai, it's crucial to note that His almighty power isn't distant or impersonal. On the contrary, He uses His power for our benefit. The same omnipotent hand that created the universe reaches into our personal lives to provide, protect, and guide.

> Whenever I am afraid, I will trust in You.
> (Psalm 56:3 NKJV)

Our human nature often causes us to doubt or fear when facing difficulties. However, knowing that El Shaddai holds all power can bring peace in these moments of uncertainty. Our weaknesses don't limit his strength; instead, His power shines brightest when we admit our need for Him.

> Those who live in the shelter of the Most High will find
> rest in the shadow of the Almighty. (Psalm 91:1 NLT)

Much like Abram, we too encounter various seasons in life. Times when our faith wavers, our hope dwindles, or the weight of the world pushes down on our shoulders.

It's in these moments that understanding God as El Shaddai becomes most pertinent.

- *In loneliness,* remember that He is sufficient to be our companion and friend.
- *In lack,* He's our provider, ensuring our essential needs are met.
- *In doubt,* He's the unwavering pillar of truth.
- *In fear,* He's the mighty one who stands beside, before, and behind us.

Trust in El Shaddai's power, especially during times of weakness and uncertainty.

As we continue our journey with El Shaddai, it's essential to remember that His power isn't just about grand miracles or dramatic displays. It's also seen in the small, everyday blessings and guidance He provides. From giving us strength to face another day to providing for our needs, His almighty power is always at work.

If you find yourself doubting God's ability to meet your needs or fulfill His promises in your life, remember Abraham and Sarah. Despite their old age and barrenness, they experienced the secret of birth because they believed in El Shaddai.

God's assertion of His almightiness was coupled with a call to Abram, "Walk before me and be blameless." It wasn't just a command but an invitation. It's as if God was saying, "Knowing that I am El Shaddai, the all-sufficient one, will you trust me fully? Will you align your life with my ways?"

Today that same call resonates in our hearts. Knowing that He is sufficient for all our needs, will we trust Him? Will we seek to walk blamelessly, understanding that His might and power are behind, before, and within us?

Take a moment to ponder the areas of your life where you've felt insufficient or overwhelmed. Bring those situations before El Shaddai. Allow His sufficiency to wash over your insufficiency.

PRAYER:

El Shaddai, God Almighty, today I recognize Your power and sufficiency. I lay down my weaknesses, doubts, and fears before You. I trust in Your might and provision. Help me walk blamelessly before You, knowing You are more than enough for every challenge I face. Amen.

Remember, as children of the Almighty God, El Shaddai, there is nothing too hard for us because there's nothing too hard for Him!

ACTION STEPS:

1. Spend time meditating on Genesis 17:1.
2. Ask God to reveal Himself as El Shaddai in your current situation.
3. Thank Him for His sufficiency, and trust Him to meet all your needs.
4. Cultivate a habit of gratitude for His daily provisions.

IMPORTANT TAKEAWAYS:

- El Shaddai is not just mighty; He is Almighty. This means there is no challenge too great for Him.
- Trusting in El Shaddai brings peace. Even when circumstances are uncertain, knowing that the Almighty God is on your side can bring comfort and reassurance.
- El Shaddai's power is evident every day. Look for signs of His work in your life daily. You'll be amazed at how He shows up.

DAY 4

ADONAI: LORD AND MASTER

> O LORD, our LORD, how majestic is your name in all the earth! You have set your glory above the heavens.
>
> —*Psalm 8:1 (NIV)*

When you gaze upon a starlit sky or stand in awe before a grand mountain, do you see the fingerprints of the master? The same God who shaped the heavens and the earth, who painted the skies and molded the mountains, is *Adonai (ah-doh-nigh)*, our Lord and master. This understanding should fill our hearts with wonder. Just as an artist leaves traces of himself in his creations, God, the ultimate artist, has infused the universe with His glory.

What's even more astounding is that this same God desires a personal relationship with each one of us. While He is the master of the universe, He also wants to be the master of our hearts. It's one thing to acknowledge God's sovereignty over creation; it's another to let Him reign supreme in our lives.

To call Him Adonai is to submit to His will, to say, "Not my will, but Yours be done." It's a conscious choice to let Him guide our steps, to trust Him in the storms, and to find rest in His promises.

Adonai signifies God's lordship over all creation and His want for an intimate relationship with us.

> The name of the LORD is a strong tower; the righteous
> run to it and are safe. (Proverbs 18:10 NKJV)

As believers seeking comfort and guidance from our Lord, we can take solace in knowing that He reigns supreme over everything—from galaxies beyond our reach to the smallest details of our lives. We can rest in His authority and trust Him with every small or large concern.

Living with the knowledge of God as our Adonai means surrendering control to Him. It's about understanding that while we have free will, choosing to live under His guidance leads to a life filled with peace and fulfillment.

However, submitting to God as Adonai may be challenging at times. Our human nature often wants to take control. But remember that surrendering doesn't mean weakness; it's a conscious choice to trust God's plan over your own.

By recognizing Him as Adonai—our Lord and master—we acknowledge His authority over our lives. Yet at the same time, we are also reminded of the intimate relationship He wants to have with us.

Acknowledging God as Adonai brings peace through trust in His sovereignty amid chaos.

Prayer is one essential way of connecting with our Adonai. It isn't just about asking for blessings and expressing gratitude for His continuous guidance throughout our lives. Prayers are conversations where we acknowledge Him as our sovereign guide.

Jesus exemplified this recognition during his prayer in Gethsemane when he said, "Father, if you are willing, take this cup from me; yet not my will, but Yours be done" (Luke 22:42 NIV),

By seeking God's will above our own, we demonstrate our trust in His lordship.

Each day, we're given opportunities to respond to His lordship. Whether through acts of obedience, moments of worship, or times of reflection, we have the chance to declare Him as our Adonai. How will you respond to His call today?

By embracing Adonai as your Lord and master, you too can experience this deeper level of intimacy with Him. It will transform your prayer life, your faith walk, and your perspective on who God truly is.

PRAYER:

Dear Adonai, our Lord and master,

Your name is majestic throughout the earth, and Your glory shines brighter than the heavens. Help me to recognize Your handiwork in creation and in my life. Draw me closer to You so I may submit to Your perfect will. Let every thought, word, and deed of mine reflect Your lordship. I surrender to You, Adonai. Reign supreme in my heart today and always. Amen.

Remember, recognizing and addressing Him as Adonai is not just about paying homage but understanding the depth of who He is—our Lord, master, and loving protector!

ACTION STEPS:

1. Spend time in prayer today acknowledging God as Adonai.
2. Pray for understanding and acceptance of God as Adonai.
3. Reflect on areas of your life where you need to surrender control to Him.
4. Share your insights with a trusted friend or mentor for accountability.

IMPORTANT TAKEAWAYS:

- Adonai signifies God's lordship over all creation and His want for an intimate relationship with us.
- Acknowledging God as Adonai brings peace through trust in His sovereignty amid chaos.
- Embrace Adonai as a loving master who guides out of affection: Understanding this will transform your relationship with God.
- Recognize that with God as your Adonai comes His commitment to care for you: This will shift your perspective from viewing God as distant to seeing Him as an intimate ally.

DAY 5

JEHOVAH: THE RELATIONAL GOD

> This is the account of the heavens and the earth when
> they were created, when the LORD God made the
> earth and the heavens.
>
> —*Genesis 2:4 (NIV)*

It's easy to feel distant from God in today's fast-paced world.
Everybody experiences periods of spiritual dryness, and feeling
disconnected from the divine is not uncommon. However, cultivating
a relationship with God is not only possible but also deeply rewarding.
Like any relationship, it requires time, effort, and understanding. If
you invest in knowing God as *Jehovah (je-ho-vah)*, it will be far easier
to experience His presence in your daily life.

In Genesis 2:4, we encounter the name Jehovah for the first time.
This name is not just a title; it reveals an aspect of God's character
that many overlook—His desire for a personal relationship with us.
Unlike other gods worshipped in ancient times who were distant and
unapproachable, Jehovah is a relational God who desires intimacy
with His creation.

This notion of a relational God is further reinforced when we
consider that after creating man and woman, He walked in the Garden

of Eden seeking their company (Genesis 3:8 NIV). In addition, throughout history, He consistently makes covenants—agreements based on mutual consent and commitment—with individuals like Abraham, Moses, and David.

Understand that Jehovah is a relational God who wants to have a personal relationship with you.

Many people believe they need to reach a certain level of spiritual maturity or righteousness before they can approach God. This idea could not be further from the truth! In fact, the Bible tells us that "while we were still sinners, Christ died for us" (Romans 5:8 NIV). This shows the depth of Jehovah's love and His longing for a relationship with us.

When you grasp this truth and begin seeing Jehovah as your loving Father rather than an impersonal deity far removed from your daily struggles, you unlock a new dimension of faith. It's like discovering an oasis in the middle of a desert—refreshing, life-giving, and utterly transformative.

Just as Adam found a companion in Eve, we find companionship with God Himself through Jesus Christ. His sacrifice bridges the gap between humanity and divinity, allowing us to experience the depth of God's love on a personal level.

Understanding Jehovah as a relational God can profoundly impact how we view ourselves and others. It challenges us to value relationships deeply—not just with each other but also with our Creator. And it reminds us that even in times of loneliness or hardship, we are never truly alone because Jehovah is always reaching out to connect with us.

Embrace Jehovah's love for you as the foundation of your relationship with Him.

But how do we cultivate this relationship? The answer comes from communication—prayer and reading His Word. Just as human relationships thrive on communication, so does our relationship with

Jehovah. Prayer is more than reciting words; it's about opening up your heart before Jehovah—sharing your joys, fears, dreams, and anxieties openly without fear of judgment or condemnation. The apostle Paul advised believers in Philippians 4:6–7 (NLT), "Don't worry about anything; instead, pray about everything. Tell God what you need, and thank him for all he has done. Then you will experience God's peace, which exceeds anything we can understand. His peace will guard your hearts and minds as you live in Christ Jesus."

As we pray and read the Bible, we get to know Him better, understand His will for our lives, and experience His love more profoundly.

> Draw near to God and He will draw near to you.
> Cleanse your hands, you sinners; and purify your
> hearts, you double-minded. (James 4:8 NKJV)

As you continue to build your relationship with Jehovah, remember that it's not about religious rituals or ticking off a spiritual checklist. It's about knowing Him personally and experiencing His love on a daily basis.

Don't be discouraged if you're struggling or feel distant from Him. He is patient and merciful. Start small by setting aside regular quiet times for prayer and Bible study, which will allow you space to listen and talk to Jehovah.

PRAYER:

Jehovah Elohim, thank You for being a God who created the heavens and the earth and desires a personal relationship with me. Help me to recognize Your hand in my life daily and to foster a deeper relationship with You. Remind me of Your faithfulness and Your promises. Let me find comfort and strength in knowing You are not just Elohim, the powerful Creator, but also Jehovah, the God who is ever-present in my life. In Jesus's name, I pray, Amen.

Remember that cultivating a relationship with Jehovah is not about religious rituals but knowing Him personally and experiencing His love daily.

ACTION STEPS:

1. Reflect on God's character as revealed in His name, Jehovah.
2. In prayer, share your thoughts, fears, joys, and struggles with God.
3. Seek godly counsel when faced with challenges.

IMPORTANT TAKEAWAYS:

- Understand that Jehovah is a relational God who desires intimacy with you.
- Embrace Jehovah's love for you as the foundation of your relationship with Him.
- Cultivate your relationship with Jehovah through regular communication—prayer and Bible reading.
- Don't be discouraged by challenges; instead use them as opportunities to grow closer to God.
- Knowing Jehovah personally brings peace and joy into our lives.

DAY 6

JEHOVAH JIREH: THE LORD WILL PROVIDE

> So Abraham called that place The LORD Will
> Provide. And to this day it is said, On the mountain
> of the Lord it will be provided.
>
> —*Genesis 22:14 (NIV)*

Abraham's journey to Mount Moriah with Isaac was no ordinary journey. It was a test of faith, obedience, and trust in God's promises. With every step Abraham took, he demonstrated unparalleled faith, believing that even if he sacrificed Isaac, God could raise him from the dead.

Just when all hope seemed lost, God stepped in with a provision—a ram caught in a thicket. This wasn't a random provision but a perfect one at the right place and the right time. *Jehovah Jireh (jeh-ho-vah jy-reh)* doesn't just provide; He provides perfectly according to our needs.

> And my God shall supply all your needs according to
> His riches in glory by Christ Jesus. (Philippians 4:19
> NKJV)

Jehovah Jireh, one of the many names of God, translates to *the Lord will provide*. Abraham first used this name when he was about to sacrifice his son Isaac on Mount Moriah. As we learned in the story, Abraham looked up, and there in a thicket, he saw a ram caught by its horns. He went over and took the ram and sacrificed it as a burnt offering instead of his son. The narrative speaks volumes about God's character, His love for us, and His ability to provide for our needs.

When we say that God is Jehovah Jireh, we acknowledge He is our source and provider. It means trusting Him even when circumstances seem impossible or dire. It signifies our faith in His divine providence—that He will always come through for us at the right time with what we need.

Trusting in Jehovah Jireh means believing God will provide for your needs at the right time.

Fast-forward thousands of years, and we see Jesus feeding five thousand people with just five loaves and two fish—another testament to God's provision. This secret shows us that God's provision isn't limited by our human understanding or resources. It's a powerful reminder that when we place what little we have in God's hands, He can multiply it to meet the needs of many.

> And God will generously provide all you need. Then you will always have everything you need and plenty left over to share with others. (2 Corinthians 9:8 NLT)

When you understand Jehovah Jireh as your provider, it changes how you view your resources. Your job, skills, and assets are not yours but gifts from God, who is your ultimate provider. Understanding this can liberate you from worry or fear related to lack or loss because no matter what happens, you know who holds everything.

Seeing God as Jehovah Jireh shifts your perspective on your resources—they're not truly yours but gifts from God, who is your ultimate source.

Understanding Jehovah Jireh can also help us navigate difficult seasons. When we face financial hardship or loss, it's easy to panic or despair. But knowing our provider allows us peace even amidst storms. It doesn't mean problems won't come; instead, it assures us of a constant *helper* through those challenges.

As you go about your day, reflect on the areas of your life where you need God's provision. It might be a financial need, relational healing, wisdom for a decision, or peace in the midst of chaos. Remember, Jehovah Jireh is not just the God who provided in the past, but He continues to provide for us today.

Are there areas in your life where you're holding back, not trusting God fully? Remember Abraham's example and consider taking a step of faith and trusting that Jehovah Jireh will meet you right where you are. Trust is foundational when it comes to believing in God's provision.

When we trust Him fully with our lives, we open ourselves up for His blessings.

PRAYER:

Jehovah Jireh, thank You for being my provider. Just as You provided for Abraham in his moment of need, I trust You will provide for me. Help me to have the faith to believe in Your promises and to trust in Your timing. I surrender my worries and anxieties to You, knowing that You see my needs even before I'm aware of them. Thank You for the ultimate provision in Christ Jesus. In His name, I pray. Amen.

In every season and circumstance, let Jehovah Jireh be your anchor. As the God who sees and provides, He is intimately acquainted with our needs. Trust in Him, for He is faithful to fulfill His promises and provide for His children.

ACTION STEPS:

1. Reflect on past instances where God has provided for your needs.
1. Spend time each day thanking Him for His provision.
2. Trust Him with your future, knowing He will provide according to His perfect plan and timing.
3. Practice generosity as an act of faith in God's providence.

IMPORTANT TAKEAWAYS:

- Trusting in Jehovah Jireh means believing He will provide at the right time.
- Seeing God as your source shifts your perspective on your resources—they're gifts from Him.
- When we place what little we have in God's hands, He can multiply it.
- Generosity becomes natural when we see ourselves as stewards rather than owners.

DAY 7

JEHOVAH RAPHA: THE LORD WHO HEALS

> He said, "If you listen carefully to the voice of the LORD your God and do what is right in his eyes, if you pay attention to his commands and keep all his decrees, I will not bring on you any of the diseases I brought on the Egyptians, for I am the LORD, who heals you."
>
> — *Exodus 15:26 NIV*

In the wake of a miraculous escape from Egypt, the Israelites found themselves in the wilderness, and with it came a new set of challenges. Bitter waters at Marah made them undrinkable, and the people grumbled. Here God revealed another facet of His character to His people: *Jehovah Rapha (jeh-ho-vah raf-ah), the Lord who heals.*

God showed Moses a piece of wood, which, when thrown into the waters, made them sweet. This immediate physical solution wasn't just about quenching thirst but a profound demonstration of God's power to heal and restore what seemed irreparable.

In life, we all face trials that leave us wounded and scarred. Be it physical pain, emotional trauma, or spiritual dryness, these are experiences we can't avoid. However, in these times of suffering and pain, remember Jehovah Rapha—the Lord who heals.

Jehovah Rapha's healing isn't limited to physical ailments. God desires to heal the broken-hearted, mend shattered spirits, and bring restoration to our souls. Our spiritual and emotional wounds, the scars left by life's battles, are within His realm of healing.

> He heals the broken-hearted and bandages their wounds. (Psalm 147:3 NLT)

While doctors and medicines play crucial roles, our ultimate healer is Jehovah Rapha. He knows our frame, understands every cell in our body, and has a deep compassion for our infirmities. Like a skilled surgeon, He can pinpoint the root of our physical and spiritual issues and bring about complete healing.

God has a solution for every problem you face. No matter how bitter your circumstances may seem, Jehovah Rapha can make them sweet again.

But healing isn't always instantaneous; sometimes it's a process that needs patience and faith on our part. The Israelites didn't get healed instantly from their thirst but had to wait until Moses found the tree and threw it into the water before they could drink.

If you find yourself doubting God's ability or willingness to heal you, remember He sees the bigger picture and knows what's best for you.

> For as the heavens are higher than the earth, So are My ways higher than your ways, And My Thoughts you're your thoughts. (Isaiah 55:9 NKJV)

Sometimes our trials serve a greater purpose—shaping our character and drawing us closer to Him.

Healing takes time. Don't rush the process; instead, trust Jehovah Rapha's timing because His timing is perfect.

Reflect on areas of your life where you need healing. Is it a physical ailment or a heart burdened with the weight of past mistakes? Is it emotional wounds from betrayal or loss? Bring these before Jehovah Rapha today. Trust in His power and His desire to bring healing to you.

Moreover, remember that healing sometimes comes in unexpected ways. It might be immediate, or it might be a journey. It might be through miracles, or it might be through the hands of doctors. But in all ways, Jehovah Rapha is at work.

Prayer is a powerful tool for invoking God's healing touch upon your life. In times of sickness or distress, praying fervently daily can bring comfort and promote recovery.

> And the prayer offered in faith will make the sick person well; the LORD will raise them up. If he has sinned he will be forgiven. (James 5:15 NIV)

Therefore, trust in Jehovah Rapha and His ability to heal as you pray with absolute faith.

PRAYER:

Jehovah Rapha, my healer, I come before You with a heart seeking restoration. I believe in Your power to heal, mend, and restore. Touch my physical body, heal my emotional wounds, and restore my spirit. Give me the patience to wait on Your timing and the faith to believe in Your methods. Thank You for being the great physician, always ready to heal and restore. In the precious name of Jesus, I pray. Amen.

Believing in Jehovah Rapha is about more than just hoping for physical health; it's understanding that God is able and willing to provide healing in every aspect of our lives—be it spiritual, emotional, or mental wounds we carry.

ACTION STEPS:

1. Pray specifically using the name Jehovah Rapha.
2. Believe in His ability and willingness to heal you.
3. Be patient, trust in His timing, and accept His will.

IMPORTANT TAKEAWAYS:

- *Healing comes in different forms.* Healing may not always be instantaneous or come in the form we expect, but we can trust God's wisdom.
- *Faith is the key.* Believing in God's ability to heal is crucial when invoking the name of Jehovah Rapha.
- *Healing takes time.* Trust in His perfect timing.
- *Remember.* No matter what you're going through right now, there is hope because we serve a God who heals—Jehovah Rapha!

DAY 8

JEHOVAH NISSI: THE LORD IS MY BANNER

And Moses built an altar and called its name, The-LORD-Is-My-Banner.

—*Exodus 17:15 (NKJV)*

Life's battles can be trickier than expected because of their unpredictability. The obstacles loom large, and the enemy appears invincible. It's like walking into a battlefield blindfolded. In such times, it's easy to feel defeated even before the battle has begun. But as Christians, we are not alone in our struggles. We have a God who fights for us—*Jehovah Nissi (jeh-ho-vah nis-see)*.

Jehovah Nissi is derived from Exodus 17:15, where Moses built an altar after a victorious battle and named it The Lord Is My Banner. This was not just a celebration of victory but also an acknowledgment that it was God who had given them the triumph.

To fully grasp this title's depth, we must venture back to the scene described in Exodus 17. The Israelites, freshly delivered from the bondage of Egypt, faced the Amalekites in the desert of Rephidim. As long as Moses held up his hands, Israel prevailed, but when he lowered them, Amalek prevailed. With the support of Aaron and Hur, Moses's hands remained steady, and Joshua defeated the Amalekite army.

In ancient times, a banner was more than just a piece of cloth. It was a rallying point for troops in the heat of battle, a symbol of unity and identity, and a declaration of allegiance. In naming the altar Jehovah Nissi, Moses affirmed that God was their unifying symbol, their protector in battle, and the one under whose authority they marched.

> The Lord will fight for you; you need only to be still.
> (Exodus 14:14 NIV)

Life is filled with challenges that can leave us feeling overwhelmed and defeated. But remember this: your victory comes from acknowledging God as Jehovah Nissi—the Lord is your banner. Understanding Jehovah Nissi as your banner means acknowledging God's protection and guidance in your life. It's about surrendering your battles to Him and trusting He will lead you to victory.

Our victories are not ours alone; they belong to God.

When we understand this truth, our perspective toward challenges changes dramatically. Instead of being intimidated by what stands before us, we can look up to God, who is above all things. As our banner, He goes before us into every battle, ensuring victory.

But how do we raise this banner? How do we invoke Jehovah Nissi in our lives? It starts with a sincere, heartfelt prayer acknowledging Him as our only hope and salvation.

Start each day with prayer, seeking His direction for your daily life. As you spend time in the Word, let God's promises of provision and protection infuse your spirit with faith and strength.

Prayer connects us with God on a deeper level, allowing His peace to fill us despite what's happening around us. It serves as a reminder that no matter how big our problems may be, they're never too big for God.

However, there might be times when you pray but don't see immediate results. Don't be discouraged. Remember, God's timing is perfect. He knows when it's best to intervene.

Prayer is the means through which we raise Jehovah Nissi over our battles.

Try incorporating scriptures in your prayers—scriptures like Psalm 20:1–5 (NIV), which says,

> May the Lord answer you when you are in distress; may the name of the God of Jacob protect you. May he send you help from the sanctuary and grant you support from Zion. May he remember all your sacrifices and accept your burnt offerings. May he give you the desire of your heart and make all your plans succeed. We will shout for joy when you are victorious and will lift up our banners in the name of our God.

PRAYER:

Jehovah Nissi, my Lord and Banner, under Your emblem, I find strength and protection. As I face the battles of life, remind me always that You go before me, stand beside me, and rally behind me. I declare my allegiance to You and find assurance in Your ever-present help. In Your victorious name, I pray. Amen.

Life is filled with challenges that can leave us feeling overwhelmed and defeated. But remember this: your victory comes from acknowledging God as Jehovah Nissi—the Lord is your banner.

By understanding this aspect of God's nature and applying it through prayer and faith, you can confidently navigate life's battles, knowing that God is guiding you toward victory.

ACTION STEPS:

1. Identify a battle or challenge you're currently facing.
2. Pray about it and acknowledge Jehovah Nissi as your banner.
3. Surrender your worries and fears to God.
4. Trust that God will fight for you and give you victory.

IMPORTANT TAKEAWAYS:

- ❧ Our victories belong to God; we are simply participants in His triumphs.
- ❧ Prayer is not just a religious routine but a powerful weapon that invokes the presence of Jehovah Nissi in our battles.
- ❧ Even when results aren't immediate, keep praying because God's timing is always perfect.
- ❧ Surrender control to God. Trusting in Jehovah Nissi means letting go of trying to control everything and allowing God's will to prevail in your life.

DAY 9

JEHOVAH MAGEN: THE LORD MY SHIELD

> Blessed are you, O Israel! Who is like you, a people saved by the LORD? He is your shield and helper and your glorious sword. Your enemies will cower before you, and you will trample down their high places.
>
> —*Deuteronomy 33:29 (NIV)*

Deuteronomy 33 is a song of blessing. Just before his passing, Moses blessed the children of Israel tribe by tribe. The culmination of these blessings paints a picture of a people divinely protected and exalted. Central to this protection is the imagery of God as a shield.

The Israelites had faced, and would continue to face, numerous enemies and challenges in their journey to and within the Promised Land. Yet the promise was clear that the Lord was their shield and their defense against all adversities.

In ancient warfare, a shield was essential to a soldier's armor. It defended against arrows, spears, and direct blows from enemies. A shield provided coverage, ensuring safety in the heat of battle.

In the mission of faith, we often encounter trials and tribulations that test our resolve. We are often confronted with arrows—unexpected challenges, hurtful words, distressing circumstances, or spiritual attacks.

The storms may rage, and the winds may blow, but a safe haven is available to us. That sanctuary is found in *Jehovah Magen (jeh-ho-vah mah-gen)*—the Lord our shield.

> God is our refuge and strength, an ever-present help in trouble. (Psalm 46:1 NIV)

The concept of God as a shield isn't just about protection from physical harm. It also extends to spiritual warfare and emotional distress. When we feel overwhelmed by anxiety or fear, when doubt creeps into our hearts, Jehovah Magen stands ready to defend us.

The Lord my Shield is not merely a metaphorical phrase; it encapsulates the essence of divine protection available to us all. When you embrace Jehovah Magen, you enlist the ultimate protector who will guard you against all adversities.

A crucial principle here is understanding that God's protection isn't limited to certain situations or specific persons. It extends to everyone who believes in Him and seeks His guidance and defense.

Jehovah Magen provides physical protection and guards us against spiritual warfare and emotional distress.

As believers, it's essential to understand that this divine shielding isn't passive or automatic. We must actively seek refuge in God through prayer, worship, and meditation on His Word. Within His presence lies safety beyond human comprehension.

> God's way is perfect. All the LORD's promises prove true. He is a shield for all who look to him for protection. (2 Samuel 22:31 NLT)

When life's challenges seem too great for us to bear alone, remember this comforting truth—you are not alone! Our loving

Father promises never to leave nor forsake those who trust in Him (Hebrews 13:5 NIV). So let your heart find rest in Jehovah Magen—your ultimate protector.

In times of adversity or uncertainty, seeking refuge in Jehovah Magen brings comfort and peace.

As believers in Christ, we must always remember that our strength comes from the Lord. He is our refuge and fortress, our ever-present help in times of trouble. By embracing Jehovah Magen—the Lord my shield—we're not just acknowledging a biblical concept but welcoming an all-encompassing divine defense system into our lives.

As we explore the depth of Jehovah Magen's protection, let's make sure we remember that He also equips us to withstand life's battles.

We are given the armor of God (Ephesians 6:10–18 NIV), each piece symbolizing a critical aspect of our faith walk—truth, righteousness, peace, faith, salvation, and the Word of God.

If you find yourself struggling to feel protected or safe despite understanding Jehovah Magen's role in your life, remember to put on this spiritual armor daily. It is there for our benefit—a divine provision from our loving Father.

PRAYER:

Jehovah Magen, my Lord and shield, I take refuge in You. Amid my battles and challenges, I am assured of Your protective covering. Guard my heart from despair, my mind from fear, and my soul from weariness. I am confident that with You as my shield, no harm can befall me. I rest in Your protection and declare Your name as my ultimate defense. Amen.

By understanding and embracing Jehovah Magen—the Lord your shield—you'll not only navigate life's storms but also experience peace and security that comes from divine protection.

ACTION STEPS:

1. Acknowledge God's sovereignty over everything else.
2. Embrace Jehovah Magen for comprehensive divine protection.
3. Put on the full armor of God every day.
4. Trust fully in His promises—believe that He is with you always.

IMPORTANT TAKEAWAYS:

- ✑ Trusting in God's sovereignty means acknowledging His control over every circumstance in your life. Whether it's a personal struggle or a global crisis, nothing happens outside His awareness or authority.
- ✑ Seeking refuge actively in Him brings comfort and peace amid adversity.
- ✑ Immerse yourself in scriptures related to divine protection.
- ✑ Putting on the full armor of God equips us for spiritual warfare—it's an essential part of embracing Jehovah Magen's protection.

DAY 10

JEHOVAH TSIDKENU: THE LORD OUR RIGHTEOUSNESS

> And this will be his name: "The Lord is Our Righteousness." In that day Judah will be saved, and Israel will live in safety.
>
> —*Jeremiah 23:6 (NLT)*

Understanding *Jehovah Tsidkenu (jeh-ho-vah tsid-keh-noo)* or *the Lord our righteousness* brings a powerful transformation to our spiritual journey. In Hebrew, Tsidkenu comes from a root word that means *straightness*. It refers to a moral and ethical standard of conduct that is straight, not crooked or twisted. When we refer to God as Jehovah Tsidkenu, we acknowledge Him as the ultimate standard of righteousness.

Jeremiah prophesied during one of the most tumultuous periods in Israel's history. Amid moral decay, false prophets, and looming threats of captivity, the message of hope emerged. Jehovah Tsidkenu promised a coming era and a future Davidic king under whose reign righteousness would be established, and Israel would live in safety and peace.

This prophecy points beyond the immediate future of Jeremiah's days and speaks of Jesus Christ, our ultimate king and Savior. Through Christ, righteousness is not just a distant ideal but a present reality for all who believe.

RIGHTEOUSNESS GIFTED, NOT EARNED

In our human nature, we often strive to earn our righteousness through good deeds, moral behavior, or religious rituals. Yet the truth remains that we can never attain the righteousness God requires on our own. This is where Jehovah Tsidkenu shines brightly. Our righteousness comes not from our actions but from God Himself.

> God made him who had no sin to be sin for us, so that
> in him we might become the righteousness of God.
> (2 Corinthians 5:21 NIV)

Jesus, through His sacrificial death and resurrection, bridges the gap between our sinful nature and God's perfect standards. By accepting Jesus as our Savior, we receive His righteousness imputed onto us like a cloak covering all our sins, making us acceptable before God's sight. Therefore, it's not about striving to achieve righteousness but rather receiving it through faith in Christ.

Through faith in Christ, we receive His righteousness, making us acceptable before God.

As we navigate our Christian journey, it's important to remember that our righteousness comes from Christ alone. We don't earn it; we receive it as a gift of grace. Understanding this relieves us from trying to achieve perfection through our own efforts and instead allows us to rest in Jesus's finished work on the cross.

> For it is by grace you have been saved, through faith—
> and this not from yourselves; it is the gift of God—
> not by works, so that no one can boast. (Ephesians
> 2:8–9 NIV)

The implications of God as our righteousness are profound:

- *In guilt,* Jehovah Tsidkenu reminds us that we are forgiven and redeemed.
- *In inadequacy,* He becomes our sufficiency, covering our imperfections.
- *In uncertainty,* He is our unwavering standard of truth and justice.
- *In relationships,* we can confidently approach God, knowing we are righteous in His eyes.

If you struggle with feelings of unworthiness or guilt over past mistakes, remember Jehovah Tsidkenu—the Lord our righteousness. Your worth is not based on your performance but on Christ's righteousness imputed onto you.

PRAYER:

Jehovah Tsidkenu, my Lord and righteousness, I am in awe of Your gift. Thank you for covering my sins, shortcomings, and inadequacies with Your perfect righteousness. I rest in the knowledge that I am righteous in Your eyes, not by my merit, but by the sacrifice of Jesus Christ. Help me to walk confidently in this identity and to reflect Your righteousness in my daily life. Amen.

Recognize that perfection isn't attainable on your own; we are made righteous through God's grace. In Him, we find rest from our striving and peace in His perfect righteousness.

ACTION STEPS:

1. Seek God through prayer.
2. Confess any sins and ask for God's forgiveness, knowing He is faithful and just to forgive.

3. Regularly thank Jesus for His sacrifice that made you righteous before God.
4. Reflect on ways you can live out this received righteousness in your daily interactions.

IMPORTANT TAKEAWAYS:

- ❧ Understanding Jehovah Tsidkenu goes beyond religious rituals; it involves delving deeper into God's character.
- ❧ Our righteousness comes through faith in Christ. It's not something we achieve by ourselves but a gift given freely by grace through faith.
- ❧ A deeper understanding of Jehovah Tsidkenu can lead to higher levels of life satisfaction and well-being.
- ❧ Reflecting God's righteousness in our actions is integral to honoring Him.

DAY 11

JEHOVAH SABAOTH: THE LORD OF HOST

> David said to the Philistine, "You come against me
> with sword and spear and javelin, but I come against
> you in the name of the Lord Almighty, the God of
> the armies of Israel, whom you have defied."
>
> —*1 Samuel 17:45 (NIV)*

The setting of 1 Samuel 17 is iconic—a young shepherd boy named
David standing against the colossal giant Goliath. Armed not with
impressive weaponry but with unwavering faith, David confronts
his adversary not in his strength, but in the name of *Jehovah Sabaoth
(jeh-ho-vah sah-bah-oth)*.

This wasn't merely a battle of physical prowess but a spiritual
warfare where God's sovereignty was being challenged. By invoking
Jehovah Sabaoth, David acknowledged that God wasn't just a local
deity but the commander of cosmic armies, both seen and unseen.

Jehovah Sabaoth is a Hebrew name for God that translates to *the
Lord of armies*. This name signifies God's supreme power over every
force in the universe. When we call upon Jehovah Sabaoth, we are
calling upon a God who commands legions of angels and has never
lost a battle.

> The LORD of hosts is with us; The God of Jacob is
> our refuge. (Psalm 46:7 NKJV)

In 1 Samuel 17:45, David declares his faith in Jehovah Sabaoth before he faces Goliath. Despite being young and inexperienced compared to Goliath's stature and prowess as a seasoned warrior, David was confident because he knew who was fighting for him.

We can learn from David's example when facing seemingly insurmountable life challenges. Instead of focusing on how large or intimidating your problem appears to be—whether it's financial trouble, illness, or relationship issues—focus on the size and mightiness of your God.

Jehovah Sabaoth reminds us that no matter how big our battles may be, our God is bigger.

In contemporary Christianity, we often downplay this militaristic image in favor of more comforting portrayals of God. We tend to see Him primarily as a loving Father or a merciful Savior but overlook His might and majesty as the Lord of hosts.

Yet the Bible doesn't shy away from presenting God as a warrior. In fact, it repeatedly emphasizes His role in fighting for His people and delivering them from their enemies.

Despite its initial introduction in 1 Samuel, the name Jehovah Sabaoth is used over 200 times throughout the Bible, predominantly in prophetic books like Isaiah and Jeremiah. It typically appears in contexts where people face insurmountable odds or dire circumstances—situations that need divine intervention on a grand scale. By invoking Jehovah Sabaoth, these biblical figures acknowledged their dependence on God's power to overcome their challenges.

> Be strong and courageous. Do not be afraid or
> terrified because of them, for the LORD your God

goes with you; he will never leave you nor forsake you. (Deuteronomy 31:6 NIV)

Facing Goliaths on life's battlefield can be overwhelming, but remember that you are not fighting alone. If you find yourself struggling with fear or doubt, pray for faith like David's. Ask Jehovah Sabaoth to fill you with courage and confidence in His power.

When praying, use the name Jehovah Sabaoth when you need divine intervention in seemingly impossible situations. This reinforces your faith in God's ability to deliver you from any circumstance. Calling upon Jehovah Sabaoth is a powerful reminder of God's promise to fight for us, providing spiritual nourishment when facing daunting obstacles.

Like David against Goliath, when we put our trust in Jehovah Sabaoth, victory becomes inevitable irrespective of the odds stacked against us.

Pause and think about the *giants* you're facing today. Consider how your life could change if you started recognizing God not just as your provider or protector but also as your mighty warrior. Imagine facing life's battles armed with the knowledge that the commander of heaven's armies is fighting for you.

How can the understanding of Jehovah Sabaoth change your perspective on these challenges? Know that you're backed by the Lord of infinite armies, turning the tide of battle in your favor.

Remember this: In every battle you face, you're not alone. Jehovah Sabaoth is on your side.

When facing battles in life, it is crucial to recognize this divine authority and draw strength from it. Just like David did when he faced Goliath, knowing that Jehovah Sabaoth is on your side can provide comfort and assurance during challenging times.

PRAYER:

Jehovah Sabaoth, Lord of hosts, I stand in awe of Your power and might. I am humbled to know that the commander of the celestial armies is on my side. I surrender my battles to You, confident in Your victory. Strengthen my faith, help me to see challenges through the lens of Your sovereignty, and lead me in a triumphant procession. Amen.

Step into your day with the boldness of David, knowing that Jehovah Sabaoth goes before you. The Lord of hosts is on your side, and no giant stands a chance in His name.

ACTION STEPS:

1. Identify the Goliaths in your life.
2. Declare your trust in Jehovah Sabaoth through prayer.
3. Meditate on scripture passages about God's mightiness.
4. Practice daily worship to keep your focus on God rather than your problems.

IMPORTANT TAKEAWAYS:

- Expand your understanding of God by embracing Him as Jehovah Sabaoth.
- Like David against Goliath, victory becomes inevitable when we trust Jehovah Sabaoth. This encourages us not to focus on the size or difficulty of our problem but instead concentrate on the size and mightiness of our God.
- Recognize that Jehovah Sabaoth is fighting for you no matter what battle you're facing.
- Understand that acknowledging God as a warrior complements rather than contradicts His other attributes like love and mercy.

DAY 12

EL ROI: THE GOD WHO SEES ME

> She gave this name to the Lord who spoke to her:
> "You are the God who sees me," for she said, "I have
> now seen the One who sees me."
> —*Genesis 16:13 (NIV)*

When understanding God's character, it's easy to think of Him as a distant deity, far removed from our daily struggles. This perspective is often born out of God's sheer magnitude and omnipotence. However, this viewpoint doesn't fully capture the depth and intimacy of God's relationship with us. There is a more personal and profound way to understand Him.

In the Bible, we find various names for God that reveal different aspects of His character. One such name is *El Roi (el roh-ee)*—the God who sees me. Hagar first used this name in Genesis 16:13 when she was in desperate circumstances, feeling alone and unseen. But God saw her distress and came to her aid.

The backdrop to this divine revelation is a desert, a place of barrenness and isolation. Hagar, a maidservant, is fleeing from the mistreatment of her mistress Sarai. Pregnant and alone, the weight of her predicament bore down on her. Yet it was here in this desolate place that the angel of the Lord found her, offering hope, direction, and a promise of a future for her unborn son.

In her overwhelming gratitude and amazement, Hagar named the place Beer Lahai Roi, which means *well of the living one who sees me*, and proclaimed the name El Roi.

You're never invisible to El Roi. He sees your struggles, your pain, your joys, and your victories.

During those times when you feel overlooked or insignificant in the grand scheme of things, remember that El Roi sees you. You are not just another face in the crowd to Him; you are uniquely created and deeply loved. El Roi is a testament to the intimate nature of God. He is not a distant deity, unconcerned with the intricacies of our lives. Instead, He is deeply involved, caring about every moment, every tear, every joy, and every sorrow.

The idea that an all-powerful being takes a personal interest in each of us can be difficult for some people to accept. It contradicts our human understanding of power dynamics, where those at the top often overlook those at the bottom. But this is where we see a fundamental difference between human leaders and our divine Creator.

Worldly standards don't determine your worth; it's established by El Roi, who values you beyond measure.

The Bible tells us that even before we were born, God knew us (Jeremiah 1:5). This means He has been intimately involved in every aspect of our lives from conception onward. It's not just a theological concept but a reality evidenced throughout scripture.

> The Lord does not look at the things man looks at.
> Man looks at the outward appearance, but the LORD
> looks at the heart. (1 Samuel 16:7 NIV)

El Roi does not merely observe us from afar; He intimately knows us. In Psalm 139, David beautifully describes how thoroughly God knows us—our actions, thoughts, and words—even before they come into existence! Our struggles do not escape His notice. Instead, they draw His compassionate attention toward us.

Even more comforting is knowing that El Roi doesn't just see our suffering; He acts on our behalf too! Later on, in the story when Hagar was in the wilderness without water for her son Ishmael (Genesis 21), it was God who heard Ishmael's cries and provided a well for them to drink from.

OUR JOURNEY

In our journey through life, we often find ourselves in our own *deserts*—places of isolation, despair, or confusion.

In these moments, the revelation of El Roi can be our oasis:

- *In loneliness*, He sees and knows your heart's longing for connection.
- *In despair*, He witnesses your pain and offers comfort.
- *In joy*, He rejoices with you, celebrating every victory.
- *In decisions*, He observes your steps and provides guidance.

The comfort that comes from knowing we serve a God who sees us can be empowering. It reassures us in our moments of solitude, strengthens us in times of hardship, and fills us with hope when despair threatens to overwhelm us.

ENGAGING DAILY WITH EL ROI:

Engaging daily with El Roi involves acknowledging His constant presence in your life. Prayer should be more than just presenting requests or expressing gratitude; it should also involve quiet moments of reflection where you acknowledge God's attentive gaze upon your life. Remember you are seen by an all-knowing God who understands your struggles and delights in your victories. He is not distant or indifferent but intimately involved in every aspect of your life.

PRAYER:

El Roi, the God who sees me, I am comforted to know that I am never out of Your sight. You are there in my moments of joy and seasons of pain. Help me always to remember that I am seen and valued by You. In times of desertion, may I find solace in Your ever-watchful eye, knowing that Your plans for me are born out of love and care. Amen.

Move forward in your day with the profound understanding that the Almighty sees you. In His gaze, you will find love, purpose, and direction. El Roi is watching over you every step of the way.

ACTION STEPS:

1. Spend fifteen minutes each day in quiet reflection or prayer.
2. Meditate on scriptures that speak of God's all-seeing nature.
3. Share your struggles with a trusted friend or mentor who can provide spiritual guidance.

IMPORTANT TAKEAWAYS:

- ❧ You are never invisible to El Roi—remember even when you feel overlooked by others, God always sees you.
- ❧ El Roi intimately knows your every struggle—your pain doesn't go unnoticed by God; He is intimately aware of what you're going through.

- ❧ Trusting in El Roi's vision can reduce stress and anxiety— knowing someone greater is watching over us provides immense comfort during challenging times.
- ❧ Spending time in prayer and scripture reading can deepen your relationship with El Roi—this helps remind us of His ever-watchful presence and love for us.

DAY 13

IMMANUEL: GOD WITH US

> The virgin will be with child and will give birth to a
> son, and they will call him Immanuel—which means,
> "God with us."
>
> —*Matthew 1:23 (NIV)*

Immanuel (*ih-man-yoo-el*), God with us. This simple phrase carries
an extraordinary promise. It signifies that God is not distant or
indifferent to our lives. Instead, He chose to dwell among us, sharing
our joys and sorrows.

As Christians, we often forget this profound truth. We become
so engrossed in our worries and fears that we overlook His constant
presence. But remember this: even when we feel alone or abandoned
by those around us, God remains steadfastly by our side.

In Psalm 139:7–10 (NIV), David acknowledges that there's no
place where he could escape from God's spirit or presence. This
realization brings both comfort and accountability. Knowing God
is always with you can provide solace during difficult times while
prompting you to live righteously.

In every season of life, the promise of Immanuel offers profound
implications:

- *In loneliness,* we are never truly alone, for God is with us.
- *In celebration,* our joys are magnified, knowing He celebrates with us.
- *In sorrow,* his comforting presence envelops us, offering solace and hope.
- *In temptation,* He understands our struggles, having faced them, and provides strength to overcome them.

Even in our loneliest moments, we are never truly alone because God is always with us.

Just think about it. The Creator of the universe cares so much about each one of us that He chose to dwell among His creation through Jesus Christ. And even after Jesus ascended into heaven, He sent the Holy Spirit to guide and comfort believers everywhere.

In John 14:16–17 (NLT) Jesus promises to send another advocate—the Holy Spirit—who would dwell within His followers forever. So not only did God live among people through Jesus Christ, but He also continues to live within those who believe in Him today!

As believers in Christ, we carry the very presence of God within us through the Holy Spirit.

However, recognizing God's presence isn't always easy. Life can be overwhelming, and our problems may seem more significant than all of us. But remember the story of David in the Bible. Even when he faced enormous challenges like fighting Goliath or running from King Saul, he was confident because he knew God was with him.

If you're having trouble sensing God's presence in your life, try setting aside some quiet time each day to pray and read His word. Ask Him to make His presence known to you in tangible ways.

Be still, and know that I am God. (Psalm 46:10 NIV)

Living out the truth of Immanuel needs intentionality on our part. Remember to be aware of God's presence as you work through your spiritual journey. It's easy to get caught up in the hustle and bustle of life and forget this essential truth. Regular prayer, meditation on scripture, and mindful living can help foster this awareness.

Immanuel carries a powerful promise—it declares that we are never alone because God is always with us. This understanding can transform your daily life by bringing peace even amidst turmoil.

PRAYER:

Immanuel, God with us, my heart overflows with gratitude for Your enduring presence in my life. Knowing that You are beside me brings unparalleled comfort and strength in moments of joy, sorrow, doubt, and celebration. May I always remain aware of Your presence, finding peace and purpose in the shadow of Your wings. Amen.

As you navigate the complexities of the day, may you be grounded in the profound reality of Immanuel. No matter where you go or what you face, God is with you today and always.

ACTION STEPS:

1. Spend daily quiet time meditating on scriptures that highlight God's presence.
2. Keep a gratitude journal.
3. Cultivate mindfulness in your daily activities.

IMPORTANT TAKEAWAYS:

ᕀ Remember that God is steadfastly by our side even when we feel alone or abandoned by those around us.

- ❧ As believers in Christ, we carry the very presence of God within us through the Holy Spirit.
- ❧ Embrace the reality that God is present in your everyday life: This truth brings comfort during challenging times and encourages righteous living.

DAY 14

EL EMUNAH: THE FAITHFUL GOD

> Understand, therefore, that the LORD your God is indeed God. He is the faithful God who keeps his covenant for a thousand generations and lavishes his unfailing love on those who love him and obey his commands.
>
> —*Deuteronomy 7:9 NLT*

Deuteronomy, a book rich with instruction and reflection, reminds the Israelites of God's faithfulness as they stand on the brink of the Promised Land. The journey had been long, interspersed with moments of faith, doubt, obedience, and rebellion. Yet one constant remained throughout their wanderings: *El Emunah (el eh-moo-nah)*, the faithful God.

He wasn't just faithful when they were obedient; His faithfulness was a pillar even during their moments of unbelief. God's commitment to His covenant was (and is) unyielding.

This divine attribute of faithfulness is more than just a comforting idea; it's an essential aspect of our relationship with Him. Understanding this can help us maintain faith even during times of uncertainty or hardship.

This realization brings both comfort and accountability. Knowing God is always with you can provide solace during difficult times while prompting you to live righteously.

Understanding that our God is El Emunah—the faithful God helps us trust Him more deeply and surrender ourselves fully to His will.

Today we will delve deeper into what it means to say that our God is El Emunah.

FIVE ASPECTS OF EL EMUNAH:

1. *God's promises are yes and amen.*
   Our faithful God does not make promises lightly. Every word He speaks carries power and truth. When He makes a promise, you can be sure He will fulfill it no matter how long it takes or what circumstances arise. Consider Abraham and Sarah, who waited decades for their promised son Isaac, or Joseph, who endured years in prison before becoming second-in-command in Egypt as promised in his dreams.

2. *God's love never fails.*
   Another characteristic of our faithful God is His unfailing love. Even when we fail Him, His love remains constant because it doesn't depend on us but on His character.

3. *God remembers His covenant.*
   Despite Israel's repeated disobedience throughout history, our faithful God never forgets His covenant made with them—from Abraham to Moses to David—promising to bless them if they obeyed Him.

4. *God provides.*
   From providing manna in the wilderness to multiplying loaves and fishes for thousands, stories abound throughout

scripture showcasing how our faithful God meets needs abundantly.

5. *God protects.*

    Whether delivering Daniel from lions or Shadrach, Meshach, and Abednego from the fiery furnace, our faithful God is a shield to those who take refuge in Him.

El Emunah is a God who keeps His promises, loves unconditionally, remembers His covenant, provides abundantly, and protects fiercely.

When we comprehend that our God is faithful, it stirs up faith within us. We become confident in His promises and rest assured, knowing He will never leave nor forsake us. We can boldly declare like David did,

> Surely goodness and love will follow me all the days
> of my life, and I will dwell in the house of the LORD
> forever. (Psalm 23:6 NIV)

God's faithfulness isn't a passive attribute. It is active, reaching out to us in love and grace daily. Recognizing this can transform our perspective, providing a solid foundation for our faith even when things don't go as planned. Sometimes it might feel like your prayers aren't being answered or that God is silent. Remember Romans 8:28 (NIV):

> And we know that in all things God works for the
> good of those who love him, who have been called
> according to his purpose.

Trust that El Emunah is working behind the scenes for your good even when you can't see it. Trusting God during difficult times might seem like an uphill task, but understanding God as El Emunah—the faithful God—can provide comfort and hope.

It's about nurturing your relationship with Him through prayer, standing firmly on His promises, and surrendering to His will.

PRAYER:

El Emunah, faithful God, my heart rejoices in Your unending faithfulness. In times when I waver, You remain constant. In moments of despair, Your steadfast love surrounds me. Help me mirror Your faithfulness in my walk with You and others. Let my life be a testament to Your unwavering love and commitment. Amen.

The faithfulness of God is not just an ancient truth reserved for biblical narratives. It is a living, breathing reality, an anchor for our souls in the turbulent seas of life.

ACTION STEPS:

1. Recount moments in your life when you've witnessed the faithfulness of God.
2. Pray and thank God for His steadfast love and faithfulness.
3. Share your experiences and insights with fellow believers to encourage them.

IMPORTANT TAKEAWAYS:

- ❧ Trust in God's promises because He is faithful.
- ❧ Your relationship with God isn't based on your performance but on His faithfulness.
- ❧ Remember that it's not about what you do but who God is—El Emunah, the faithful God.

DAY 15

ABBA FATHER

> For you did not receive a spirit that makes you a slave again to fear, but you received the Spirit of sonship. And by him we cry, "Abba, Father."
> —*Romans 8:15 (NIV)*

In the heart of every person lies an innate desire to belong, to be understood, and to be loved unconditionally. It's this very sentiment that's encapsulated in the term *Abba (ab-bah)*, an intimate Aramaic term that children use for their fathers, similar to Daddy or Papa. Abba isn't just any title but a term of endearment, intimacy, and deep familial connection.

The God of the universe, the one who set the stars in place and formed the mountains, invites us to approach Him with the same simplicity and trust that a child approaches their loving parent. In Romans 8:15, we're reminded that our relationship with God isn't founded on fear or servitude but on love and adoption. We are chosen, beloved, and welcomed into His family.

When Jesus Christ died on the cross for us, it was more than just redemption from sin; it was an invitation to a loving family. As believers in Christ, we are adopted into God's family as His children.

Like any loving parent, He walks beside us during times of difficulty, celebrates our victories, and guides us toward fulfilling our divine purpose.

As believers in Christ, we have been adopted into God's family and can call Him Abba—daddy.

In the Bible, when Jesus prayed in Gethsemane before His crucifixion (Mark 14:36 NIV), He addressed God as Abba. "'Abba, Father,' he said, 'everything is possible for you. Take this cup from me. Yet not what I will, but what you will.'"

This wasn't a casual address; it depicted an intense emotional bond between Him and His Father. It shows us that despite facing extreme suffering and pain, Jesus found comfort in His relationship with His Father.

Just as earthly fathers provide for their children's needs out of love, so does our heavenly Father care for us. He provides for our physical needs and offers spiritual guidance and wisdom through His Word.

> For you are all children of God through faith in Christ Jesus. (Galatians 3:26 NLT)

As you grow in your faith, nurturing this intimate relationship with God is essential. Spend time daily in prayer and reading His Word. Share your joys, sorrows, fears, and hopes with Him just as you would with a loving earthly father.

If you find it difficult to see God as a loving Father due to negative experiences with your earthly father, remember that God is not like man. He will never fail or forsake us. He loves unconditionally and is always ready to listen when we call out to Him.

Understanding God as Abba Father transforms our relationship with Him from one based on fear to one rooted in love.

By seeing God as your Abba Father, you develop a deeper connection with Him. You start to understand His love for you better and feel more secure in His presence. It transforms your prayer life from a formal ritual into an intimate conversation with your heavenly dad.

Remember, prayer is not about uttering perfect words but about honest, heart-to-heart conversation. During these moments of vulnerability, we experience God's comforting presence the most.

As you grow your understanding of God as your Abba Father, you'll start to experience His love more profoundly. This will deepen your faith and bring peace and joy into your life.

PRAYER:

Dear Abba, my Father in heaven,

Thank You for adopting me into Your family, for choosing me and loving me unconditionally. Help me always to remember that I am Yours and that You are ever eager to listen to my heart's cries. Strengthen my trust in You and deepen my understanding of Your love. I am grateful to call You Abba, my Father, my protector, and my guide. Amen.

Realizing God as Abba, as a loving Father, grants us an immense sense of security and purpose. We are loved, we belong, and we have a divine destiny in His grand plan.

ACTION STEPS:

1. Spend time daily in prayer, addressing God as your Abba Father.
2. Embrace your identity as a child of God by recognizing your adoption into His family.

3. Reflect on how seeing God as your Father changes your perspective on trials and tribulations.

IMPORTANT TAKEAWAYS:

- ❧ We are adopted into God's family through Christ. Our salvation goes beyond forgiveness of sins; it also brings us into an intimate relationship with our Creator.
- ❧ Seeing God as your Abba Father can revolutionize your spiritual journey.
- ❧ If you struggle with seeing God as a loving Father due to past experiences or misconceptions, remember that human standards do not define His nature.
- ❧ Be patient with yourself. This is a journey; it takes time to grasp this reality entirely.

DAY 16

EL NOSO: THE GOD WHO FORGIVES

O LORD, our God, you answered them. You were a forgiving God to them, but punished them when they went wrong.

—Psalm 99:8 (NLT)

Each of us carries the weight of past mistakes, regrets, and sins. Sometimes the burden feels too heavy to bear, and we yearn for relief, redemption, and reassurance. In these moments of deep introspection and repentance, it's here that we encounter *El Noso (el no-so)*, the God who forgives.

The beauty of forgiveness isn't found in the act itself but in the heart of the one who extends it. Forgiveness is an expression of love, mercy, and grace. It's a reflection of God's character—a God who is willing to wipe away our transgressions and remember them no more.

In Psalm 99:8, the psalmist paints a picture of a God who answers when called upon and forgives but also ensures justice. This dual nature might seem contradictory, but it perfectly balances God's love and righteousness. He is both merciful and just.

When faced with the enormity of our mistakes, it's easy to feel unworthy or beyond redemption. But God's forgiveness is not based on our worthiness but on His love. Our role is to approach Him with a contrite heart, genuinely seeking forgiveness.

> If we confess our sins, he is faithful and just and will forgive us our sins and purify us from all unrighteousness. (1 John 1:9 NIV)

Once you embrace God's forgiveness, you're called to live in that freedom. It means letting go of guilt or shame associated with past mistakes.

It also means forgiving yourself as God has forgiven you.

El Noso's forgiveness stems from His mercy and grace rather than what we deserve.

Understanding El Noso's forgiving nature allows us to extend forgiveness to others freely. Just as He forgives us despite our shortcomings, so should we forgive others when they wrong us.

Holding onto anger or resentment only poisons our hearts and hinders our relationship with God. However hard it may be to forgive someone who has hurt you deeply, remember that Christ died for your sins while you were still a sinner (Romans 5:8).

If Jesus could do this for humanity out of love, surely we can find it within ourselves to forgive those who have wronged us.

> Be kind and compassionate to one another, forgiving each other, just as in Christ God forgave you. (Ephesians 4:32 NIV)

If you find it difficult to forgive someone who has wronged you deeply, try praying for them. Ask God to help you see them through His eyes—flawed yet loved unconditionally. This perspective may help soften your heart toward them and enable you to extend forgiveness.

Understanding El Noso's forgiving nature empowers us to forgive others freely.

Today take time to contemplate any areas of your life where you might be holding onto past mistakes or struggling to forgive someone. Bring these before El Noso, lay them down, and receive His forgiveness and peace.

Remember His mercies are new every morning, and His love is unending.

PRAYER:

El Noso, I come before You, acknowledging my transgressions and seeking Your mercy. Thank You for Your unfailing love, for seeing beyond my faults and granting me a fresh start. Fill my heart with gratitude and the capacity to forgive as I've been forgiven. Help me to walk in Your ways, reflecting Your grace and love in my daily life. Amen.

By understanding God as El Noso, we find the hope and strength to rise above our past, forging a future rooted in grace, redemption, and transformative love.

ACTION STEPS:

1. Reflect on Psalm 99:8.
2. Pray for a forgiving heart.
3. Seek God's forgiveness sincerely.
4. Forgive those who have wronged you.

IMPORTANT TAKEAWAYS:

- Recognize your fallibility and constant need for God's mercy.
- Embrace the unconditional love offered by El Noso.
- Strive to emulate His forgiveness by extending it to others.
- Walk humbly, acknowledging your dependence on divine grace.

DAY 17

CHRIST: THE ANOINTED ONE

> Simon Peter answered and said, "You are the Christ, the Son of the living God."
>
> —*Matthew 16:16 (NKJV)*

Jesus Christ (jee-zus k-rye-st) is not just another historical figure or prophet; He is God's anointed Son, chosen to bring salvation to humanity. In Matthew 16:16, Simon Peter proclaimed, "You are the Messiah, the Son of the living God." This statement resonates with profound truth that continues to shape our faith today.

In Jewish tradition, oil was used for anointing. It wasn't ordinary oil but specially prepared holy anointing oil described in Exodus 30:22–25 (NIV). The act of anointing symbolized being set apart for God's service and empowered by His Spirit.

Understanding Jesus as the Anointed One is fundamental to grasping our faith's essence. Christ comes from the Greek word Christos, which translates to Anointed One. In Old Testament times, anointing was a sacred ritual that signified being chosen by God for a specific purpose. Kings were anointed; prophets were anointed. When Peter confessed Jesus as *the Christ*, he acknowledged Him as the long-awaited Messiah, God's chosen one, whose coming had been prophesied by Old Testament prophets.

Recognizing Jesus as the Anointed One also means acknowledging His role as our high priest. Like how priests were anointed before serving in temples, God anointed Jesus to serve us by offering Himself as a perfect sacrifice for our sins on Calvary's cross.

> The next day, John saw Jesus coming toward him and said, "Look, the Lamb of God, who takes away the sin of the world!" (John 1:29 NIV)

Recognizing Jesus as Christ means acknowledging Him as Lord and Savior. It's an acceptance of His sacrifice on our behalf and a commitment to follow His teachings and embody His love.

Yet there's more to this confession than mere acknowledgment. It also signifies submission to His authority and obedience to His commands. Declaring that Jesus is Christ—the Anointed One— implies that we are ready to surrender ourselves under His lordship. Our wants no longer drive us, but we strive to fulfill His divine purpose in our lives.

This confession also calls for faith—unwavering belief in who He is despite circumstances or oppositions that may arise.

Remember how Peter made this declaration amidst disciples who were unsure about their master's identity? That's what faith looks like, affirming Jesus's divinity even when others doubt or deny it.

> I tell you, whoever publicly acknowledges me before men, the Son of Man will also acknowledge him before the angels of God. (Luke 12:8 NIV)

Having faith in Jesus as Christ—the Anointed One—is not just about vocal declarations but also involves living out this faith. It means striving to be like Him, loving the unlovable, forgiving the unforgivable, and serving with humility. This is how we genuinely honor Him as our king, high priest, and Lord.

Declaring Jesus as Christ involves surrendering ourselves completely under His reign.

Don't lose heart if you're finding it hard to live out your faith or surrender completely under His reign. You're not alone in this journey. Remember Peter? Even after his bold confession, he faltered at times, but Jesus never gave up on him.

FIVE WAYS TO EMBRACE CHRIST—THE ANNOTATED ONE:

1. *Daily prayer.* Prayer is not merely asking for things but aligning ourselves with God's will. Start your day by acknowledging Christ's lordship over your life.
2. *Bible study.* The Bible is God's love letter to us. It reveals Christ's nature and mission as the Anointed One. Regular study deepens our understanding and strengthens our faith.
3. *Worship.* Worship is an expression of love toward God. Through songs, we declare Jesus as king, priest, and prophet— recognizing His sovereignty in every aspect of our lives.
4. *Fellowship.* Fellowship with other believers helps us grow in faith. Sharing insights about Christ's anointing can enrich our collective understanding.
5. *Service.* As followers of Christ, we're called to serve others selflessly, just like He did. This way, we reflect the heart of the Anointed One to those around us.

Today, pause and reflect on the role of Jesus as the Christ in your life. Do you know Him merely as a historical figure, or is He a living, active presence in your daily walk?

Take a moment to reaffirm your faith, recognizing Jesus as the

Messiah and inviting Him to take His rightful place at the center of your heart.

PRAYER:

Dear Jesus, the Anointed One,

I thank You for being the fulfillment of all prophecies and for being the chosen one to bridge the gap between humanity and God. Open my eyes to see You not just as a figure of history but as my personal Savior. May my life reflect my allegiance to You, and may my heart always recognize and honor You as the Christ, the Son of the living God. Amen.

When we truly understand Jesus as Christ, our relationship with Him deepens. We're connected not just to a Savior from two millennia ago but to a living Messiah, ever-present and forever interceding on our behalf.

ACTION STEPS:

1. Set aside quiet time each day for prayer and meditation on the scripture.
2. Listen to Christian music or hymns that affirm Jesus's anointing.
3. Seek God's guidance in identifying your divine calling.
4. Seek ways to serve others with love and humility.

IMPORTANT TAKEAWAYS:

- Declaring Jesus as Christ implies complete surrender under His reign.
- Faith involves affirming Jesus's divinity even when others doubt or deny it.

- ❧ Living out your faith means striving to emulate Christ's love, forgiveness, and humility.
- ❧ If you falter in your walk of faith, remember that Jesus never gives up on you; He qualifies those He calls!

DAY 18

JEHOVAH SHALOM: THE LORD IS PEACE

> Peace I leave with you; my peace I give you. I do not
> give to you as the world gives. Do not let your hearts
> be troubled and do not be afraid.
>
> —*John 14:27 (NIV)*

Life is a complex journey, filled with unpredictable twists and turns.
There are times when the road becomes rocky and the journey
difficult, leading us to feel anxious and unsettled. In such moments,
it's easy to forget that we're not alone; we have *Jehovah Shalom (jeh-ho-
vah shah-lom)*—the Lord our peace.

This title for God was first used in Judges 6:24 by Gideon after he
had an encounter with God's angel. Despite the ongoing war around
him, Gideon experienced an overwhelming sense of tranquility
knowing that God was on his side.

When we feel overwhelmed by life's trials and tribulations, it's
easy to lose sight of this divine peace offered by our heavenly Father.
However, like Gideon who built an altar named Jehovah Shalom
amid a war-torn land, we too must learn to seek solace in our
relationship with God rather than focusing solely on our problems.

When it comes to finding peace in the midst of life's storms, it's really important that you avoid seeking solace in temporary fixes. Many people turn to distractions like excessive work, unhealthy relationships, or even substance abuse in an attempt to find tranquility. They believe these methods work because they provide a momentary escape from their troubles.

However, these solutions are fleeting and often leave people feeling more restless and emptier than before. The key here is understanding that peace isn't found in the absence of problems but rather in the presence of God.

> The LORD will give strength to His people; the LORD will bless his people with peace! (Psalm 29:11 NKJV)

Jehovah Shalom doesn't promise a life without storms, but He assures us of His calming presence when waves threaten to overwhelm us. It's a peace that anchors our souls, reminding us that we're never alone, no matter how fierce the battle.

Jehovah Shalom provides an unshakeable peace rooted not in circumstances but in His unwavering presence.

In the journey toward embracing Jehovah Shalom in our lives, it's important to remember that this is not merely about passive acceptance. It involves actively seeking His presence and guidance in every situation we face. It begins with surrendering our worries and fears to God and trusting Him completely with our lives.

This act of surrender frees us from the burden of trying to control everything and allows us to rest securely knowing that God is in control.

> Give all your worries and cares to God, for he cares about you. (1 Peter 5:7 NLT)

FIVE KEYS TO EXPERIENCING JEHOVAH SHALOM:

If you're struggling to find peace amidst your current circumstances, consider the following:

1. *Recognize His presence.* It all starts with acknowledging that God is present in your life. He isn't distant or detached from your experiences; instead, He walks beside you through each trial you face. Understanding this can bring a sense of calmness and stability to your life.
2. *Trust Him.* Trust goes hand in hand with faith. If you believe that God has your best interests at heart, then trust Him completely with your circumstances no matter how dire they may seem.
3. *Pray continually.* Prayer isn't just about asking for things; it's also about seeking God's guidance and wisdom in every aspect of your life.
4. *Meditate on His Word.* The Bible provides timeless wisdom and encouragement for believers facing any kind of difficulty or uncertainty.
5. *Be still.* In a world full of noise and distractions, taking time out to be still before God can provide much-needed peace and clarity.

Embracing God as Jehovah Shalom means inviting His peace into every area of our lives—our fears, our decisions, our relationships, and our uncertainties. It means leaning into Him, trusting His promises, and allowing His peace to replace our anxieties.

Even among chaos, peace can be found through faith in Jehovah Shalom.

PRAYER:

Jehovah Shalom, the Lord of peace,

In the midst of life's storms and uncertainties, I turn to You. Grant me Your peace, the peace that surpasses all understanding, to guard my heart and mind. Help me to trust in Your promises and to find rest in Your presence. May I always remember that You are my peace, my anchor, and my refuge. Amen.

By recognizing and relying on Jehovah Shalom, we find solace not just for today, but a lasting peace that carries us through all of life's challenges.

ACTION STEPS:

1. Identify any temporary fixes you've been relying on for peace.
2. Surrender these to Jehovah Shalom in prayer.
3. Regularly attend church services or fellowship gatherings for spiritual nourishment.
4. Reach out to fellow believers for support during tough times.

IMPORTANT TAKEAWAYS:

- Jehovah Shalom is our source of peace in every situation.
- Recognizing His presence is key to experiencing His peace.
- Trusting God means surrendering control of our circumstances to Him.
- Prayer and meditation on God's Word are vital spiritual disciplines for maintaining inner peace.
- Being still before God allows us space to hear from Him and receive His divine wisdom.

DAY 19

EL EMET: THE GOD OF TRUTH

Into your hands I commit my spirit; redeem me,
O LORD, God of truth.

—Psalm 31:5 (NIV)

In our daily walk with God, we often encounter His different attributes. One of the most beautiful names He carries is *El Emet (el eh-met)*—the God of truth. This name signifies that our God is true in all His ways and actions. It's a profound truth that has a lot to teach us.

When we say God is truth, it means He embodies the essence of truth in its purest form. God stays constant, unlike humans, who can sometimes be deceptive or inconsistent. Every word He speaks comes from a place of absolute honesty and integrity.

El Emet also implies reliability and trustworthiness. When life throws curveballs at us, when people let us down, or when situations become uncertain, it's comforting to know that we serve a God whose character never changes—one who stays faithful to His promises no matter what.

The beauty of serving the God of truth is not just about acknowledging this attribute but also reflecting it in our lives. We are called to live out this truth by being honest in our interactions with others, keeping our promises just as God does for us, and living lives that reflect integrity.

Understanding El Emet brings an assurance into your life, rooted in knowing that you're loved by a truthful, reliable, and unchanging Father who will always lead you on the path of righteousness for His name's sake.

> For the word of the Lord is right and true; he is faithful in all he does. (Psalm 33:4 NIV)

As Christians, understanding this aspect of God's nature can revolutionize our faith and daily walk with Him. Knowing that He is the source and standard of all truth gives us confidence to trust in His Word and promises. It assures us that what He says will come to pass because He cannot lie or break His promises.

Embrace El Emet—the embodiment of absolute truth and faithfulness.

In a world awash with shifting sands of opinions, fleeting trends, and relative truths, there's a deep-seated yearning in the human heart for something steadfast, unchanging, and trustworthy.

It's easy for us humans to get swayed by emotions or situations around us. We often tend to believe what we see or feel rather than what is actually true. But when we understand that our heavenly Father is El Emet—the God of truth—it changes everything.

We can rest assured knowing that His words are trustworthy and reliable, regardless of our circumstances.

This understanding of God as El Emet also impacts how we live our lives. It encourages us to be truthful in our dealings with others because we serve a God who values truth. It challenges us to align our lives with His word because we know it's the ultimate truth.

> But if we walk in the light as He is in the light, we have fellowship with one another, and the blood of

Jesus Christ His Son cleanses us from all sin. (1 John 1:7 NKJV)

Living as people of truth requires us to continually walk in God's light. To walk in His light means rejecting falsehood and embracing honesty—externally and internally. It involves confessing our sins before God and seeking His guidance through prayer and reading scripture.

We must let the reality that we serve a truthful God permeate every part of our existence—from how we conduct ourselves at work or school to how we interact with others personally. This means speaking the truth even when it's difficult or unpopular because doing so reflects the character of El Emet within us.

And you will know the truth, and the truth will set you free. (John 8:32 NLT)

Serving a truthful God calls for honesty and integrity in every area of life.

If you find yourself struggling to live out this truth-centered lifestyle, remember that we have the Holy Spirit who guides us into all truth (John 16:13). Ask Him for wisdom and strength to walk in truth daily.

PRAYER:

El Emet, the God of truth,

I thank You for being my unwavering foundation in a world of uncertainties. Anchor my heart to Your truths, and let Your word be a lamp unto my feet.

Help me to walk in honesty, to speak with integrity, and to live in alignment with Your righteous ways. I commit my spirit, my choices, and my path to You, O God of truth. Amen.

In a world where truth is often relative, we have the privilege of knowing and being known by El Emet, the ultimate and eternal truth. Let's cherish this relationship, seek His guidance, and aim to be reflections of His truth in the world around us.

ACTION STEPS:

1. Pray and ask El Emet to help you trust His words over your feelings.
2. Pray for wisdom to discern truth from falsehood.
3. Strive for honesty and integrity in all areas of life.

IMPORTANT TAKEAWAYS:

- ❧ Embrace El Emet as your guide in every decision you make; His words are trustworthy and reliable.
- ❧ Align your life with God's word because it's the ultimate truth.
- ❧ We are called to seek and stand for the truth amidst a deception-filled world.
- ❧ The Holy Spirit helps us live a lifestyle centered on God's truth.

DAY 20

JEHOVAH M'KADDESH: THE LORD MY SANCTIFIER

> Consecrate yourselves and be holy, because I am the
> LORD your God. Keep my decrees and follow them.
> I am the LORD, who makes you holy.
> —*Leviticus 20:7–8 (NIV)*

Holiness and sanctification often feel distant in today's fast-paced, worldly environment. Yet throughout the Bible, God calls His people to a life set apart that radiates His purity and love. This divine invitation to holiness is encapsulated in the name *Jehovah M'Kaddesh (jeh-ho-vah muh-kah-desh),* which means the Lord my sanctifier.

Sanctification is not just about avoiding certain sins or adhering to a list of rules. At its core, it's about transformation—a metamorphosis from our sinful nature to a nature reflecting God's holiness. Jehovah M'Kaddesh doesn't merely call us to be holy; He empowers, equips, and leads us into holiness. This sanctifying work is His divine action in our hearts, molding us into the image of Christ.

Sanctification isn't a single event but a lifelong process in which we continually grow closer to God and become more like Him. We are made holy by His grace, not by our own efforts or good deeds.

When we surrender ourselves fully to Him, he refines us like gold in fire, removing all impurities until only His image stays.

> May God himself, the God of peace, sanctify you through and through. May your whole spirit, soul and body be kept blameless at the coming of our Lord Jesus Christ. (1 Thessalonians 5:23 NIV)

Sanctification is a divine process initiated by God and sustained by our continual surrender to Him.

When we understand this truth about sanctification—its ongoing nature—it helps put our struggles with sin into perspective. We all have weaknesses or areas where temptation seems particularly strong. But remember that each day offers an opportunity for growth and purification through Jehovah M'Kaddesh.

God doesn't expect perfection overnight but a willing heart ready to grow in holiness daily. He knows you will stumble; what matters most is your willingness to get up again and continue on the path toward Him.

> Then Jesus said, "Come to me, all of you who are weary and carry heavy burdens, and I will give you rest. Take my yoke upon you. Let me teach you, because I am humble and gentle at heart, and you will find rest for your souls. For my yoke is easy to bear, and the burden I give you is light." (Mathew 11:28–30 NLT)

If you're struggling with embracing sanctification, here are some critical aspects about Jehovah M'Kaddesh to keep in mind:

1. *God initiates sanctification.*
    Our sanctification begins when we accept Christ as our Savior. It is God who calls us out of darkness into His

marvelous light (1 Peter 2:9). Remember that sanctification isn't something we can achieve on our own; it's a gift given freely by God.

2. *Sanctification involves surrender.*

   To be sanctified means allowing God complete control over every aspect of your life—thoughts, actions, and wants. This surrender may seem daunting initially, but remember that Jesus said his yoke is easy and his burden light (Matthew 11:30).

3. *It's a continuous process.*

   Sanctification isn't instantaneous; it's progressive and ongoing throughout our lives (Philippians 1:6). Every day presents new opportunities for growth and transformation.

4. *Sanctification leads to holiness.*

   The ultimate goal of sanctification is holiness—becoming more like Christ in thought, word, and deed (1 Peter 1:15–16). Holiness isn't about perfection but striving to live a life pleasing to God.

Understanding Jehovah M'Kaddesh helps us grasp the depth of God's love for us—He desires to save us and transform us into His likeness.

As you continue your spiritual journey, remember that it's OK not to be perfect. Our Heavenly Father isn't looking for perfection but progression. So, let go of any guilt or shame you may be carrying around because of past mistakes or current struggles. Allow Jehovah M'Kaddesh—The Lord My Sanctifier—to work in you.

PRAYER:

Jehovah M'Kaddesh, the Lord my sanctifier,
   I come before You, longing for Your transformative touch. Mold,

refine, and make me a vessel worthy of Your calling. Help me to embrace Your daily work in my life, yielding to Your sanctifying power. Let my life reflect Your holiness, bearing witness to Your grace and love. Amen.

We embark on a transformative journey by recognizing Jehovah M'Kaddesh in our lives. It's a path that challenges us, reshapes us, and ultimately leads us to a deeper, more intimate relationship with our Creator. Let's embrace His sanctifying work with open hearts, rejoicing in the promise of becoming more like Christ with each passing day.

ACTION STEPS:

1. Meditate on His Word. Reflect on scriptures that speak about holiness and sanctification.
2. Confess your sins regularly and ask God for forgiveness.
3. Be patient with yourself; sanctification is a process.

IMPORTANT TAKEAWAYS:

- Jehovah M'Kaddesh calls us to be holy as He is holy.
- Sanctification is an active pursuit, not a passive process.
- It involves building a relationship with God and surrendering our will to His will.
- Embracing sanctification can lead to a more peaceful and fulfilling life.
- Sanctification is not an overnight process but a lifelong commitment.

DAY 21

EL OLAM: THE EVERLASTING GOD

Then Abraham planted a tamarisk tree in Beersheba, and there he called on the name of the LORD, the Everlasting God.

—*Genesis 21:33 (NKJV)*

In the world we live in, change is inevitable. Seasons change, people age, and even our most cherished possessions wear out over time. But within all this transience, there is one constant: El Olam—the Everlasting God. This name of God first appears in Genesis 21:33 when Abraham calls on the name of the Lord, El Olam. It's a powerful declaration that our God exists from everlasting to everlasting.

El Olam (el oh-lahm) means *the eternal or everlasting God*. He existed before anything else and will continue to exist after everything else has passed away. This truth brings comfort because it reminds us that our heavenly Father remains unchanged no matter what changes we face in life. His love for us never wavers, His mercy never runs out, and His grace is always sufficient.

This understanding of El Olam also gives us hope during times of uncertainty or fear. When we feel overwhelmed by circumstances beyond our control, we can trust the one who holds eternity in

His hands. We are reassured knowing He sees the end from the beginning and works all things together for good.

> Every good and perfect gift is from above, coming down from the Father of the heavenly lights, who does not change like shifting shadows. (James 1:17 NIV)

The constancy of El Olam encourages us to have faith as well. Since God does not change like shifting shadows, we can rely on His promises with absolute certainty. What He has said will come to pass because He is faithful and true.

> I saw heaven standing open and there before me was a white horse, whose rider is called Faithful and True. With justice he judges and makes war. (Revelation 19:11 NIV)

Recognizing God as the everlasting one should cultivate a profound sense of trust and security in us. Though brief on this earth, our lives are held in the hands of the one who transcends time itself. We can rest, knowing that our future, our purpose, and our ultimate destiny are secure in Him.

Knowing God as El Olam provides comfort, hope, faith, and stability in a world marked by change and uncertainty.

Abraham's story is not just one from ancient times; it carries relevance even today. Every day, we face challenges that may seem insurmountable—physical illness, emotional pain, financial crisis—the list goes on. Yet in these trials, if we remember that we serve an everlasting God who sees our past, present, and future simultaneously—it can bring us immense comfort.

> His divine power has given us everything we need for life and godliness through our knowledge of him

who called us by his own glory and goodness. (2 Peter 1:3 NIV)

This verse from Peter's epistle further emphasizes how understanding God's eternal nature impacts our lives positively. It tells us that through His divine power, He provides for all our needs—physical or spiritual—for He knows what lies ahead for us.

As we circumnavigate life's complexities, we may encounter impossible situations. In such moments, remember that El Olam is not bound by time or human limitations. He can turn around any situation, no matter how hopeless it appears.

When we understand that our God is eternal, it should affect how we view Him and how we live our lives. We can rest assured knowing that His plans for us are everlasting.

Understanding El Olam helps us trust Him with every aspect of our lives because He sees beyond what we see.

God's everlasting nature is a testament to His eternal existence and His enduring promises. If He has spoken it, He will bring it to pass. Every promise, every prophecy, and every word He has said is backed by the full weight of His eternal character. This knowledge brings hope and assurance to our hearts even in the most uncertain times.

PRAYER:

El Olam, the Everlasting God,

I stand in awe of Your eternal nature, finding solace in the truth that You are unchanging. Among the temporal moments of my life, be my constant. Anchor my faith in Your eternal promises, and let my heart rest in Your everlasting embrace. Guide my days and let them be a testament to Your timeless love and grace. Amen.

As we journey through life, may our hearts be continually drawn to El Olam, the Everlasting God. In His eternal nature, we find the hope, assurance, and love that sustain us through every season.

ACTION STEPS:

1. Start your day with prayer: Ask El Olam to help you see beyond your current circumstances.
2. Reflect on instances where God has been faithful in your life.
3. Share what you've learned about El Olam with a friend or family member.

IMPORTANT TAKEAWAYS:

- Trust in God's unchanging nature.
- Rest in God's everlasting love.
- Lean on God's infinite wisdom.
- Embrace God's eternal purpose.

DAY 22

EL CHASEDDI: THE GOD OF MERCY

> In his unfailing love, my God will stand with me. He
> will let me look down in triumph on all my enemies.
> —*Psalm 59:10 (NLT)*

In the context of Psalm 59, David is in dire straits. Surrounded by
enemies and seeking refuge, he cries out to God. But David doesn't
just call on a mighty warrior or a strategic planner; he calls on *El
Chaseddi (el chas-di)*, recognizing that God's mercy will ultimately
deliver him from his foes.

When it comes to understanding the nature of God, you mustn't
fall into the trap of seeing Him as a distant, unfeeling entity. Many
people view God this way, believing He is aloof and indifferent to
our struggles. This belief often stems from personal experiences of
pain and disappointment. However, this perspective is far from the
truth. There exists a more comforting and empowering reality.

The Bible introduces us to many facets of God's character through
His different names. One such name is El Chaseddi, which translates
to the God of mercy.

This name reveals a side of God that is compassionate, forgiving, and deeply involved in our lives. It reminds us that He cares about our pain and struggles and is eager to show us mercy.

El Chaseddi isn't just a title; it's an invitation for us to experience His mercy firsthand. When we understand this aspect of God's character, we can confidently approach Him, knowing He will respond with compassion rather than condemnation.

> The Lord is compassionate and merciful, slow to get angry and filled with unfailing love. (Psalm 103:8 NLT)

God's mercy is a gift freely given, not earned or deserved.

Now here's something you might not expect: embracing the mercy of El Chaseddi doesn't mean ignoring justice or condoning sin. In fact, it's because God loves us so much that He cannot overlook our wrongdoings—they separate us from Him and lead us down destructive paths. Instead of punishing us immediately for our sins as justice would demand, He offers forgiveness through His Son, Jesus Christ—an act of incredible mercy.

David was no stranger to mistakes; he committed adultery and murder yet found forgiveness in El Chaseddi. This isn't to say that David didn't face consequences for his actions, but instead God's mercy was available even in the midst of discipline.

> Who is a God like you, who pardons sin and forgives the transgression of the remnant of his inheritance? You do not stay angry forever but delight to show mercy. You will again have compassion on us; you will tread our sins underfoot and hurl all our iniquities into the depths of the sea. (Micah 7:18–19 NIV)

El Chaseddi isn't merely a God who occasionally shows kindness. His mercy is part of His very nature. It's the force that compels Him to reach out to a lost and hurting world again and again, offering redemption, hope, and love. This underlines the inherent nature of our Father as one who dispenses grace without measure or limit.

The more intimately you know El Chaseddi, the more you understand your value in His eyes. Despite our flaws and mistakes, He sees beyond them all and loves us unconditionally. Such knowledge should empower you to live fearlessly, knowing that your worth does not fluctuate based on human judgment.

You can experience the power of El Chaseddi by inviting His mercy into your life every day. Start by acknowledging your need for His mercy and expressing your desire in prayer.

PRAYER:

El Chaseddi, God of mercy, I stand in awe of Your boundless and steadfast love. Time and again, Your mercy has been my refuge, hope, and redemption. In moments when I feel undeserving, Your mercy reminds me of Your unchanging love. Help me to extend the same mercy I receive from You to those around me. May my life be a reflection of Your merciful heart. Amen.

Embark on your day empowered in the knowledge that El Chaseddi watches over you. His mercy is new every morning, ready to meet you in every situation, guiding you with loving-kindness and infinite compassion.

ACTION STEPS:

1. Pray and ask God to help you understand and experience His mercy.
2. Extend forgiveness and show mercy toward someone who has wronged you.
3. Be patient with yourself—spiritual growth takes time.

IMPORTANT TAKEAWAYS:

- El Chaseddi reveals a side of God that is compassionate and forgiving.
- Accepting God's mercy isn't about our worthiness but His loving nature.
- We are called not only to receive but also to extend God's mercy toward others.

DAY 23

JEHOVAH SALI: THE LORD MY ROCK

> The Lord is my rock, my fortress and my deliverer;
> my God is my rock, in whom I take refuge, He is my
> shield and the horn of my salvation, my stronghold.
>
> *Psalm 18:2 (NIV)*

We often encounter challenges that threaten to throw us off balance. These situations can leave us feeling overwhelmed and uncertain about the future. But there's a solution—turning to *Jehovah Sali (jeh-ho-vah sah-lee)*, the Lord our rock. In Psalm 18:2, David referred to God as his rock, fortress, and deliverer. As Christians, we too can lean on God in this same way.

The name Jehovah Sali is derived from two Hebrew words. Jehovah, meaning *the existing one* or Lord, and Sali, which translates to *my rock*. This term embodies the idea of God as a steadfast foundation in our lives, an unchanging source of security amidst life's storms.

Jehovah Sali is more than just a name; it's an assurance of stability in times of turmoil. When everything around you seems shaky and unstable, He stays unchanging and reliable. The world may change and people may fail you, but Jehovah Sali stays constant.

When David called God his rock, he was not referring to a small stone but rather a massive, immovable mountain. This gives us an idea of how strong and dependable our God is. Just like mountains serve as landmarks because they are unmoving no matter what happens around them, so does Jehovah Sali remain unchanging in His love for us.

When life's storms come your way—be it sickness, loss, or disappointment—remember that you are not alone. Your feelings may sway like the branches of a tree in a storm, but underneath you is an immovable rock that can weather any storm. That's Jehovah Sali.

> He alone is my rock and my salvation, my fortress where I will not be shaken. My victory and honor come from God alone. He is my refuge, a rock where no enemy can reach me. (Psalm 62:6–7 NLT)

Just as a physical rock offers shelter and protection from the elements, Jehovah Sali offers spiritual shelter and protection from life's storms.

There are times when we feel overwhelmed by our circumstances. During these moments of vulnerability, it might seem easier to lean on worldly things for comfort rather than trusting in God's plan. However, these sources of comfort often prove unreliable over time. In contrast, Jehovah Sali never changes or fails us.

God's steadfastness doesn't depend on how good or bad we've been. His love for us isn't performance-based; it's unconditional and everlasting. When everything else shifts around us—our relationships, jobs, or health—Jehovah Sali stays consistent.

As we grow in our relationship with Jehovah Sali, we learn to trust Him more. Trusting God doesn't mean denying reality or ignoring the pain. It means acknowledging our situations but believing that God is greater than any circumstance we face.

Our relationship with God isn't performance-based; His love is unconditional and everlasting.

Yet a misconception exists that relying on God means passive acceptance of circumstances. On the contrary, trusting in Jehovah Sali involves active engagement with Him. It means seeking His guidance, obeying His commands, and aligning our actions with His will.

Prayer is a powerful way to connect with God and seek His guidance. Begin by acknowledging God as your rock expressing your faith in Him as the stable foundation of your life. Share your worries, fears, and anxieties with Him, knowing He is a refuge amid any storm.

PRAYER:

Jehovah Sali, my Lord and rock, I am profoundly grateful for the stability You bring into my life. You remain constant and steadfast in a world that often feels like shifting sand. Strengthen my faith, and let me always find my footing in You. When the storms of life rage, remind me that I stand secure on the solid foundation of Your love and promises. Amen.

Jehovah Sali provides stability amid life's storms. Just as a rock stays firm despite the raging waters around it, so does God remain steadfast during our trials. It's comforting knowing that no matter what happens around us or within us—whether it be fear, doubt, or despair—we have a solid foundation upon which we can stand.

ACTION STEPS:

1. When faced with challenges, pause and remind yourself of Jehovah Sali—the Lord my rock.
2. Reflect on instances where God has been your refuge during past trials.
3. In your prayers, thank Jehovah Sali as your rock.

4. Be patient—sometimes it takes time for situations to change, but remember that God is working behind the scenes.

IMPORTANT TAKEAWAYS:

- Understanding the nature of our rock gives us confidence.
- Building our lives on Christ confirms stability.
- Prayer invites divine intervention in our situations.
- Trusting in God provides peace amid turmoil.
- Worship brings us closer to Jehovah Sali and reminds us of His greatness.

DAY 24

EL DE'OT: THE GOD OF KNOWLEDGE

Do not keep talking so proudly or let your mouth speak such arrogance, for the LORD is a God who knows, and by him deeds are weighed.

—*1 Samuel 2:3 (NIV)*

This affirmation of God's knowledge emerges from the prayer of Hannah—a woman who had known deep sorrow and profound joy. After years of barrenness and heartache, she experienced God's miraculous intervention, resulting in the birth of Samuel. In her heartfelt prayer of gratitude, she acknowledges God's infinite knowledge, recognizing that nothing escapes His attention and understanding.

It's easy to forget that *El De'ot's (el-de-ot's)* knowledge extends beyond just knowing facts about us but also involves understanding the motivations behind our actions and thoughts. In 1 Samuel 2:3, Hannah acknowledges that God sees beyond outward appearances and into the heart.

Human perceptions, understanding, or biases don't limit El De'ot. He sees beyond the surface, comprehending the depths of human hearts, the reasons behind actions, and the true essence of every situation.

God sees everything—past, present, and future. He knows us intimately, every thought before it forms on our lips.

> Before a word is on my tongue you know it completely,
> O' LORD. (Psalm 139:4 NIV)

What a comfort to know that even when we feel misunderstood or alone in our struggles, there is a loving Father who understands us completely! This all-encompassing knowledge means He judges justly, loves deeply, and acts with perfect precision.

There is nothing unknown to God; His knowledge surpasses all understanding.

El De'ot doesn't just provide knowledge; He offers wisdom too. Wisdom is the application of knowledge; it helps us discern right from wrong. It guides us in making decisions that reflect our faith and values.

So how do we access this divine wisdom? It begins with humility—acknowledging that we don't know everything, and that's OK because God does. When you surrender your need for control or understanding over a situation to Him, you open up yourself to receive His divine guidance.

> Humble yourselves before the LORD, and he will lift
> you up. (James 4:10 NIV)

The next step involves actively seeking wisdom through prayer and meditation on His word. As you spend time communing with Him, He reveals bits of His infinite wisdom to you—one day at a time, one step at a time.

> If any of you lacks wisdom, you should ask God, who
> gives generously to all without finding fault, and it
> will be given to you. (James 1:5 NIV)

Accessing divine wisdom requires humility and actively pursuing God through prayer and scripture study.

Sometimes despite our best efforts, we still find ourselves confused or uncertain. In these moments, it's essential to remain patient and trust that God is working things out for your good. His timing is always perfect, and He will reveal the answers when you're ready to receive them.

Don't be discouraged if you encounter trickier problems or feel like you're not receiving the guidance you need. Continue seeking Him fervently and maintain an open heart. Consider seeking godly counsel from trusted spiritual leaders or mentors who can provide additional insights.

> For the LORD gives wisdom; from His mouth come knowledge and understanding. (Proverbs 2:6 NKJV)

In our journey, recognizing God as El De'ot brings comfort and guidance:

- *In confusion,* He offers clarity as He knows the end from the beginning.
- *In decision-making,* His knowledge provides direction and wisdom.
- *In repentance,* knowing He sees our heart's true intent brings genuine reconciliation.
- *In prayer,* our words are known even before they are spoken, allowing authentic communion with Him.

PRAYER:

El De'ot, God of knowledge, I am humbled and comforted that You understand everything. In moments of confusion, be my clarity. When I face decisions, grant me wisdom drawn from Your perfect knowledge. Help me to walk with integrity, knowing that my heart and actions are always visible to You. I trust in Your all-encompassing understanding and find peace in Your perfect judgments. Amen.

Embrace today with the profound awareness that El De'ot walks with you. His infinite knowledge illuminates your path, understands your heart, and guides your steps with divine precision.

ACTION STEPS:

1. Acknowledge your limitations and surrender them to God.
2. Recognize that nothing is hidden from El De'ot.
3. Spend time daily in prayer and studying scripture.
4. Seek godly counsel when faced with complex issues.

IMPORTANT TAKEAWAYS:

- There is nothing unknown to God; His knowledge surpasses all understanding.
- Accessing divine wisdom requires humility and actively pursuing God through prayer and scripture study.
- Patience is crucial as God reveals His wisdom in His perfect timing.
- Seeking godly counsel can provide additional insights when dealing with complex issues.

DAY 25

EL HAKKAVOD: THE GOD OF GLORY

> The voice of the Lord echoes above the sea. The
> God of glory thunders. The LORD thunders over
> the mighty sea.
>
> —*Psalm 29:3 (NLT)*

As the day dawns, illuminating the world in radiant splendor, we are drawn into the majesty and wonder of a name that resounds throughout the heavens and earth: *El Hakkavod (el hak-kah-vod)*, the God of glory.

Psalm 29 is a magnificent hymn of praise, drawing our attention to the powerful and majestic voice of the Lord. It paints a picture of God's glory manifesting in nature—thunderstorms, mighty waters, and shaking forests. These grand displays of nature are but a whisper of His infinite glory, a gentle reminder of His omnipotent presence.

God's glory is all around us. It's in the sunsets that paint the sky with brilliant hues each evening, in the stars that twinkle far above our reach, even in the simplest flower blooming by your feet. These are all reflections of His splendor.

> The heavens declare the glory of God; the skies
> proclaim the work of his hands. (Psalm 19:1 NIV)

The Hebrew word for glory, *kavod*, originally means *weight* or *heaviness*. This suggests that God's glory is substantial; it carries weight in our lives and isn't superficial or fleeting. To acknowledge God as El Hakkavod is to recognize His overwhelming magnificence and the weight of His presence. It affirms that He is worthy of awe, reverence, and exaltation.

When we refer to Him as El Hakkavod, we thank His supremacy over everything in existence—from the smallest atom to the largest galaxy.

We also recognize His absolute authority in our lives. Our response should be one of worship and surrender because He is worthy of all honor.

> And they were calling to one another: "Holy, holy, holy is the Lord Almighty; the whole earth is full of his glory." (Isaiah 6:3 NIV)

Understanding El Hakkavod deepens our appreciation for God's omnipotence and majesty reflected in nature and everyday life.

El Hakkavod isn't just about experiencing God's glory but also revealing it to others. Jesus says in Matthew 5:16 (NIV), "In the same way, let your light shine before men, that they may see your good deeds and praise your Father which in heaven."

This implies we should live in such a way that our actions reflect God's love and goodness, compelling others toward Him. Reflecting God's glory is about living a life that is transformed by the love of Christ, and that bears witness to the grace, love, and truth of God. It involves personal transformation and active engagement in the world to share God's love and truth with others. So how can we live in a way that glorifies El Hakkavod?

SEVEN DAILY PRACTICES TO GLORIFY EL HAKKAVOD:

1. *Start your day with praise.* Every morning before you start your routine, take time to praise God for who He is—the God of glory.
2. *Live righteously.* Strive to live righteously each day by following biblical principles.
3. *Be humble.* Acknowledge your dependence on Him constantly.
4. *Serve others selflessly.* Show love toward others by serving them selflessly.
5. *Pray continually.* Maintain an attitude of prayer throughout your day.
6. *Share your faith.* Don't hesitate to share your faith and experiences with others.
7. *End your day with gratitude.* Every night, express gratitude for His guidance throughout the day.

Recognizing God as El Hakkavod is not just about acknowledging His majesty but also living a life that reflects His glory. This doesn't mean we have to be perfect—after all, we are humans prone to mistakes. But it does mean striving each day to live in a way that brings honor to Him.

PRAYER:

El Hakkavod, God of glory, I stand in awe of Your magnificent splendor. The vastness of the universe, the beauty of nature, and the depth of love all echo Your glorious presence. Help me to live in a manner that reflects Your glory, to worship with genuine reverence, and always to recognize the weight of Your holy presence in my life. May my every action, word, and thought bring glory to Your name. Amen.

Step into your day with a heightened sense of wonder, knowing that El Hakkavod surrounds you. In every sunbeam, every raindrop, and every act of kindness, catch a glimpse of the God of glory and let your life resonate with His splendid majesty.

ACTION STEPS:

1. Meditate on scriptures about God's glory.
2. Spend quiet time in nature observing the beauty around you.
3. Put on worship music and sing praises to the God of glory.

IMPORTANT TAKEAWAYS:

- Understanding El Hakkavod deepens our connection with God.
- Recognizing Him as the God of glory calls for consistent worship and surrender.
- Living righteously, serving selflessly, and praying continually are among the practices that glorify Him.
- Sharing our faith helps spread His glory further.
- Even when we stumble, striving each day to honor Him is what truly matters.

DAY 26

EL HAKKADOSH: THE HOLY GOD

> But the LORD Almighty will be exalted by his justice, and the holy God will show himself holy by his righteousness.
>
> —*Isaiah 5:16 (NIV)*

Isaiah, the prophet, penned these words in the context of a divine lament over the unfaithfulness of Israel. Even as the people turned away, God's inherent holiness remained a stark contrast to the world's ways. Isaiah reminds us that God's holiness will always shine through, made evident by His righteous acts and unwavering justice.

In our journey of faith, one of the most profound aspects to grasp is understanding God as *El Hakkadosh (el hak-kah-dosh)*, which translates to *the Holy God*. This name paints a picture of a deity that is not only set apart but also pure and righteous in all His ways. When we approach Him with this understanding, our relationship with Him takes on a deeper meaning.

Holiness, in its essence, is about separateness and purity. To say God is holy is to recognize that He is distinct from His creation, unparalleled in His purity, righteousness, and perfection. El

Hakkadosh is untouched by sin, corruption, or imperfection. We see this divine holiness in the book of Revelations, where John the disciple describes the scene of God's throne in heaven,

> Each of the four living creatures had six wings and was covered with eyes all around, even under his wings. Day and night, they never stop saying: "Holy, holy, holy is the Lord God Almighty, who was and is, and is to come." (Revelations 4:8 NIV)

When we comprehend how holy God is, it changes how we approach Him in prayer and worship. It fosters a more profound reverence and awe for Him, leading to a deeper and more intimate relationship with our Creator.

God's holiness is absolute and unchanging. Embrace El Hakkadosh as an integral part of your spiritual journey.

As we continue to explore El Hakkadosh, it's essential to remember that His holiness isn't meant to distance us from Him. Instead, it invites us into a closer relationship. It calls us toward sanctification—the process of becoming more like Christ.

> Give the following instructions to the entire community of Israel. You must be holy because I, the LORD your God, am holy. (Leviticus 19:2 NLT)

Embracing the essence of El Hakkadosh—the Holy One—is pivotal in deepening your relationship with God. Recognizing His divine nature and righteousness enables us to understand Him better while guiding us toward a more meaningful Christian walk.

It involves embodying values such as love, kindness, and humility that reflect His character. It means aligning our actions with His righteousness and striving each day to live a life pleasing to Him. Embracing the truth of God as El Hakkadosh shapes our daily walk:

- *In worship,* our adoration takes on a deeper reverence, knowing we approach a Holy God.
- *In repentance,* we are reminded of the gravity of sin and the beauty of His forgiveness.
- *In living,* our daily actions become a pursuit of holiness, mirroring His character.
- *In relationships,* we seek to love and interact with others in ways that reflect God's purity.

The fear of the LORD is the beginning of wisdom,
And the knowledge of the Holy One is understanding.
(Proverbs 9:10 NKJV)

By seeking wisdom through fearing (revering) our Lord's holiness, we gain more profound insight into His character and intentions for us.

However, our comprehension of El Hakkadosh shouldn't make us afraid of God but rather inspire awe and holy fear (or reverence) within us because even though God is perfectly holy, He still loves us. This love was demonstrated when He sent His son Jesus Christ to die for our sins so we could be reconciled with Him.

If you find it challenging to grasp this concept or feel overwhelmed by God's holiness, don't be discouraged. Remember that it's not about achieving perfection but about growing in understanding and love for El Hakkadosh. Remember that the Holy Spirit is always there to guide and help you.

By understanding this divine aspect of our Lord and incorporating it into your devotions and actions, you will not only enrich your spiritual journey but indeed live a life that glorifies El Hakaddosh—the Holy God.

PRAYER:

El Hakkadosh, Holy God, I stand in awe of Your perfect purity and righteousness. You are distinct, separate from all imperfections, and unmatched in Your holiness. I am humbled by Your grace that allows me to approach You. Instill in me a heart that seeks holiness, that I might reflect Your character in every facet of my life. Help me to live in a manner worthy of Your calling, honoring You as the Holy God in all I do. Amen.

As you journey through the day, let the holiness of El Hakkadosh be your guiding light. Seek to reflect His purity in your actions, words, and thoughts, honoring the Holy God who loves you immeasurably.

ACTION STEPS:

1. *Reflect on God's Words.* Reading scriptures highlighting God's holiness can deepen your understanding and appreciation for His divine nature.
2. *Pray with reverence.* Approach your prayers with deep respect and awe for who God truly is—El Hakkadosh.
3. *Live righteously.* Strive to live in alignment with God's teachings, mirroring His righteousness in our actions.

IMPORTANT TAKEAWAYS:

- El Hakkadosh signifies the Holy God. His holiness is absolute and unchanging.
- Understanding the holy nature of God deepens your relationship with Him.
- We are called to mirror this divine sanctity in our lives.

❧ Despite our imperfections, El Hakkadosh loves us unconditionally.

❧ The Holy Spirit guides us toward leading a life reflective of God's holiness.

DAY 27

EL RACHUM: THE GOD OF COMPASSION AND MERCY

> For the LORD your God is a merciful God; He will not abandon or destroy you or forget the solemn covenant He made with your ancestors.
>
> —*Deuteronomy 4:31 (NLT)*

In Deuteronomy, Moses speaks to the Israelites, recounting God's faithfulness and urging them to obedience. Even as he warns them against turning from God, Moses reminds them of the nature of their heavenly Father—*El Rachum (el rah-khoom)*. Though they might face consequences for their actions, God's compassion and mercy ensure that He will never utterly forsake them.

Our understanding of compassion becomes more profound when viewed through the lens of divine mercy. The Bible paints many portraits of people who experienced this firsthand: David found mercy after his adulterous affair with Bathsheba, Peter was forgiven despite denying Christ three times, and Paul received grace even though he persecuted Christians before his conversion.

God's compassion and mercy aren't fleeting emotions or reactions. They form the very heartbeat of His nature. To understand El Rachum is to recognize that His love goes beyond mere obligation or duty—it's a profound, boundless love that feels, understands, and acts on our behalf.

Delving deeper into this understanding of God's compassionate nature allows us to see how it manifests in everyday life. Consider moments when you've been shown kindness undeserved or when grace has been extended even when punishment was due. These instances echo El Rachum's character—a kind-hearted Father willing to forgive His children time after time. He understands our weaknesses and is ready to extend mercy when we falter.

> Because of the Lord's great love we are not consumed,
> for his compassions never fail. They are new every
> morning; great is your faithfulness. (Lamentations
> 3:22–23 NIV)

El Rachum sees beyond your flaws; He looks at your heart and offers compassion where others may offer judgment.

Jesus Christ, the incarnate Son of God, perfectly exemplified compassion and mercy during His time on earth. He healed the sick, comforted the grieving, forgave sinners, and ultimately, laid down His life for humanity. In following Christ, we are called to mirror His actions, showing compassion and mercy to both friends and enemies, those alike and different from us, and those who can and cannot repay us.

Living out compassion and mercy involves both attitude and action. We must cultivate a heart that is tender toward others, seeing them through the eyes of Christ and being moved to act on their behalf. This might involve providing physical aid, offering a listening ear, or extending forgiveness. Importantly, our acts of compassion and mercy should not depend on others' responses; instead they should flow out of a genuine love for God and people.

When we live out compassion and mercy, we participate in God's redemptive work in the world. These acts have the power to transform lives, mend broken relationships, and reflect the kingdom of God on earth. Furthermore, as we practice compassion and mercy, we ourselves are transformed, becoming more like Christ and deepening our relationship with El Rachum.

> Be kind and compassionate to one another, forgiving each other, just as in Christ God forgave you. (Ephesians 4:32 NIV)

Reflecting God's compassion and mercy is not optional for followers of Christ; it is a vital part of our calling and an expression of our love for God. As we seek to embody El Rachum in our daily lives, we become conduits of His love and grace, demonstrating to a watching world the transformative power of divine compassion and mercy.

Let us, therefore, commit to living as reflections of El Rachum, tirelessly seeking to show compassion and mercy to all we encounter.

- *In mistakes,* His mercy offers grace, a second chance to rise and move forward.
- *In pain,* His compassion enfolds us, providing solace and healing.
- *In gratitude,* we acknowledge the countless mercies we receive, often unseen or unspoken.
- *In service,* empowered by His love, we extend compassion and mercy to those around us.

When we show compassion and mercy toward others, we are transformed, becoming more like Christ and deepening our relationship with El Rachum— the God of compassion and mercy.

PRAYER:

El Rachum, God of compassion and mercy, Your love astounds me. In moments when I feel undeserving, You envelop me in Your mercy.

When my heart aches, Your compassion meets me, soothing and restoring. Help me not only receive but also extend Your compassion and mercy to others. May my life be a reflection of Your tender heart, drawing others to Your embrace. Amen.

As you go about your day, let these truths sink deep into your heart. Let them guide your actions and shape your perspective on God, yourself, and those around you.

ACTION STEPS:

1. Reflect on instances where God has shown His compassion in your life.
2. Pray for a heart that mirrors Christ's compassion.
3. Extend this divine compassion toward others; show kindness even when undeserved.

IMPORTANT TAKEAWAYS:

- Understanding our need for mercy is the first step toward experiencing El Rachum.
- Acceptance of forgiveness frees us from guilt and shame.
- Regular repentance keeps our hearts receptive to divine correction.
- Showing compassion reflects our understanding of Christ's sacrifice for us.
- Trusting in God's faithfulness assures us of His constant supply of fresh mercies.

DAY 28

JEHOVAH ORI: THE LORD MY LIGHT

> The LORD is my light and my salvation; Whom shall I fear? The LORD is the strength of my life; Of whom shall I be afraid?
>
> —*Psalm 27:1 (NKJV)*

Imagine you're in the middle of a dense forest with thick trees blocking most of the sunlight. You've been wandering for hours, but you can't find your way out. Suddenly you see a flicker of light in the distance. As you move toward it, the path becomes more evident. Before long, you emerge from the forest into a beautiful meadow bathed in sunlight.

This is how life can feel sometimes—like we're lost in a dark forest with no way out. But just as light guided you through that forest, so too can God's presence guide us through our darkest moments.

In Hebrew tradition, each name given to God carries unique significance and reveals different aspects of His character. When we refer to Him as *Jehovah Ori (jeh-ho-vah or-ee)*—the Lord my light—we acknowledge His role as our guide and protector.

Light has many properties—it reveals truth, provides warmth,

112

promotes growth, and enables sight. Similarly God brings truth to our lives by showing what's hidden in darkness. He warms us with His love, nurtures spiritual growth, and gives us insight into situations beyond our comprehension.

Just as physical light impacts our daily lives significantly—guiding us through traffic or helping us avoid obstacles on footpaths—God's spiritual light plays an equally vital role in navigating our spiritual journey.

> Your word is a lamp to my feet and a light for my path. (Psalm 119:105 NIV)

In a world where shadows of doubt, fear, and despair often loom, Jehovah Ori stands as a beacon of hope, guidance, and assurance.

Sometimes we might feel as if God's light is not shining on us. We may even question whether He is there at all. But remember that even the darkest night will end, and the sun will rise. God's light never truly leaves us; it's often our perception that changes based on circumstances.

So how do we ensure that this divine light continues to shine upon us? It begins with faith—believing that even in your darkest hour, God will illuminate your path because He has promised never to leave nor forsake you (Hebrews 13:5). Faith triggers obedience, opening avenues for His guidance.

> We walk by faith, not by sight. (2 Corinthians 5:7 NIV)

Walking by faith invites us into a deeper communion with the Creator, a relationship not based on sight but on trust. It calls us to fix our eyes not on what is seen but on what is unseen, for what is seen is temporary, but what is unseen is eternal (2 Corinthians 4:18). In the unseen, we find a wellspring of hope, a foundation of strength, and a reservoir of peace.

In a world that demands evidence that craves the security of the known, walking by faith is an act of radical defiance. It is choosing to step forward when the road ahead is shrouded in mystery, trusting in a God whose promises are sure, even when the evidence is not immediately apparent.

> Now faith is being sure of what we hope for and certain of what we do not see. (Hebrews 11:1 NIV)

However, faith is not devoid of questions or moments of doubt. Like the father who cried out to Jesus, "I believe; help my unbelief!" (Mark 9:24), we, too, navigate the delicate balance between faith and doubt, belief and uncertainty.

But in these moments of vulnerability, we discover that faith is not the absence of doubt but the presence of belief in doubt. It is the choice to cling to the promises of God even when the storms of life rage and the waves of uncertainty crash around us.

That is why it is essential to know and understand God as Jehovah Ori—the Lord my light. When we say God is our light, we acknowledge that He illuminates our path and helps us see clearly through life's dark times.

At the end of it all, embracing Jehovah Ori means letting go of fear and stepping into faith, recognizing that even when life gets dark, there's a divine light guiding our path.

PRAYER:

Jehovah Ori, Lord my light, in moments of darkness, Your radiant presence guides and comforts me. Help me to always turn toward Your light, seeking guidance, clarity, and hope. As I navigate life's challenges, may I remain ever aware of Your illuminating presence, and may my life reflect Your light to those around me. Amen.

By understanding and applying Jehovah Ori—the Lord my light—in your life, not only will you navigate life's darkest times with confidence but also radiate His divine light onto others around you.

ACTION STEPS:

1. Acknowledge your need for God every day.
2. Share all your cares with Him because He cares for you.
3. Trust in God's guidance instead of leaning on your own understanding.

IMPORTANT TAKEAWAYS:

- Jehovah Ori illuminates our path and reveals hidden truths in dark times.
- Experiencing His guidance requires faith followed by obedience.
- Even in periods of doubt or confusion, persistently seek Him through prayer and scripture reading.

DAY 29

RUACH HAKKODESH: HOLY SPIRIT

> Do not cast me from your presence or take your Holy
> Spirit from me.
>
> —*Psalm 51:11 (NIV)*

Psalm 51 captures the raw and intimate plea of King David following his grave sins of adultery and murder. Recognizing the weight of his actions, he doesn't just ask for forgiveness; he fears the departure of God's very presence in his life. More than the loss of kingdom or crown, David dreads the absence of the Holy Spirit, a testament to the Spirit's preciousness.

The term *ruach* in Hebrew can be translated as *breath* or *wind*, symbolizing life, power, and movement. The Holy Spirit, the *Ruach Hakkodesh (roo-ahkh ha-koh-desh)*, is God's breath in us, empowering, guiding, and transforming us from within. He is the Spirit that convicts, comforts, and leads us into all truth.

The Holy Spirit is not an *it* but a *who*. The Holy Spirit is the third person of the Holy Trinity and sits alongside God the Father and God the Son (Jesus Christ) in perfect harmony—the oneness of God—three in one.

The Holy Spirit is God's presence in the world today, working in the lives of believers. The Holy Spirit plays a crucial role in the life of a Christian, guiding, teaching, empowering, and transforming us from the inside out. The work of the Holy Spirit is vital for living a life that is pleasing to God and for being an effective witness of the Gospel in the world.

The Holy Spirit guides us on the path of righteousness and helps us make decisions that align with God's plan for our lives.

The Holy Spirit plays many roles in our lives as believers. As Jesus said in John 14:26 (NKJV), "But the Helper, the Holy Spirit, whom the Father will send in My name, will teach you all things." From guiding us into truth to comforting us during trials, His influence is pervasive and indispensable. It's crucial that we actively seek His guidance daily.

KEY ASPECTS OF THE HOLY SPIRIT'S ROLE IN A CHRISTIAN'S LIFE:

1. *Teacher and guide*

    The Holy Spirit teaches believers and helps them remember the teachings of Jesus (John 14:26). He guides them in all truth and provides wisdom and understanding of God's Word (John 16:13).

2. *Comforter and helper*

    Jesus referred to the Holy Spirit as the helper or comforter (Greek: paraclete), meaning one who comes alongside to assist and provide comfort (John 14:16, 26; 15:26).

3. *Convicter of sin*

    The Holy Spirit convicts people of their sins and their need for salvation through Jesus Christ (John 16:8).

4. *Empowerment*

   Believers receive power when the Holy Spirit comes upon them, empowering them to be witnesses for Christ (Acts 1:8).

5. *Giver of gifts*

   The Holy Spirit gives spiritual gifts to believers for the building up of the Church and for the common good (1 Corinthians 12:7–11).

6. *Fruit producer*

   The *fruit of the Spirit* (love, joy, peace, patience, kindness, goodness, faithfulness, gentleness, and self-control) are produced in the lives of believers as they live in step with the Holy Spirit (Galatians 5:22–23).

7. *Intercessor*

   The Holy Spirit helps believers in their weakness, interceding for them with groanings too deep for words (Romans 8:26).

8. *Seal and guarantee*

   The Holy Spirit serves as a seal in the lives of believers, a guarantee of their inheritance and redemption as God's own (Ephesians 1:13–14; 2 Corinthians 1:22).

9. *Sanctifier*

   The Holy Spirit works to sanctify believers, making them holy and conforming them to the image of Christ (2 Thessalonians 2:13; Romans 8:29).

10. *Bearer of God's presence*

    The Holy Spirit is God's presence dwelling within believers, making their bodies a temple of the Holy Spirit (1 Corinthians 6:19)—an equally vital role in navigating our spiritual journey.

Now it's easier to understand why King David pleaded with God so desperately not to take His Holy Spirit from him. Psalm 51:11 underscores how vital the Holy Spirit was to David.

Embracing the Ruach Hakkodesh means acknowledging His presence in your life daily—seeking His guidance, comfort, and empowerment regularly.

If you're struggling to understand or experience the Holy Spirit, don't despair. Start by praying for a fresh revelation of His presence. Spend time in worship and allow yourself to be open to His leading. Remember it's not about striving but surrendering.

PRAYER:

Ruach Hakkodesh, Holy Spirit, I treasure Your presence in my life. Breathe afresh in me, renewing my spirit and aligning my heart with the Father's. Guide my steps, empower my actions, and mold my character to reflect Christ. I long for a deeper communion with You, to hear Your whispers and feel Your guiding hand in every aspect of my life. Amen.

Step into your day with the profound awareness that you are not alone. Ruach Hakkodesh, the Holy Spirit, dwells within you, guiding, empowering, and transforming you into the likeness of Christ with every breath you take.

ACTION STEPS:

1. Pray for a deeper understanding of the Holy Spirit.
2. Meditate on scriptures that talk about the Holy Spirit.
3. Be open and responsive to His leading in your daily life.

IMPORTANT TAKEAWAYS:

- ✺ The Holy Spirit is a *who* and not an *it*, an equal part of the Trinity.
- ✺ Cultivating our relationship with God involves nurturing our connection with His Spirit.
- ✺ The Holy Spirit plays an active role in your spiritual life.

DAY 30

ALPHA AND OMEGA: GOD OF BEGINNING AND END

I am the Alpha and the Omega, the Beginning and
the End, the First and the Last.

—*Revelation 22:13 (NKJV)*

Alpha (al-fuh) is the first letter of the Greek alphabet while *Omega
(oh-may-guh)* is the last; symbolically they signify completeness.
When used together as alpha and omega, they represent an eternal
continuum—a divine entity without beginning or ending, precisely
what God represents.

The reason why we often struggle with accepting the concept
of God as both the alpha and omega is that our human minds
are conditioned to perceive time in a linear fashion. This limited
perspective can make it difficult for us to grasp the infinite nature of
God fully. However, understanding this aspect of His character can
bring profound peace and assurance in our lives.

God's eternal nature means that He exists outside of time. He was
present before creation, He is actively involved in our lives today, and
He will continue to be there in the future. This timeless existence
allows Him to see the bigger picture we often miss. He knows our

past, understands our present struggles, and has already seen our future victories.

When we accept Jesus Christ as our personal Savior, we enter into an everlasting relationship with Him, who is both alpha and omega. Our lives become part of His grand narrative—one that starts with creation and ends with eternal life. This realization should guide our decisions, shape our values, and give us hope in times of trouble.

> Jesus Christ is the same yesterday, today, and forever. (Hebrews 13:8 NKJV)

Embrace this truth: God is not bound by time or space. His love for you began before you were born and will continue throughout eternity.

God's role as both alpha and omega also means that He has complete control over every situation in your life. Nothing happens without His knowledge or permission. Even when circumstances seem chaotic or out of control, remember that God is still sovereign.

> Are not two sparrows sold for a penny? Yet not one of them will fall to the ground apart from the will of your Father. And even the very hairs of your head are all numbered. (Matthew 10:29–30 NIV)

In life, there are seasons of beginnings (alpha) and endings (omega). Understanding that God is present in both can help us navigate these transitions with grace and faith. When one door closes, another opens, but often, we look so long at the closed door that we do not see the one that has opened for us.

As we face trials and tribulations in life, it's essential to remember that God is always with us. It's not about denying the realities of life or being overly spiritual. It's about acknowledging His sovereignty over our lives and trusting Him to guide us through the twists and turns. He knows our beginning, end, and everything in between.

But blessed are those who trusts in the LORD and have made the LORD their hope and confidence. They are like a trees planted along the riverbank, with roots that reach deep into the water. Such trees are not bothered by the heat or worried by long months of drought. Their leaves remain green, and they never stop producing fruit. (Jeremiah 17:7–8 NLT)

Remember this, in every ending lies a new beginning; trust God to guide you through these transitions.

PRAYER:

Alpha and Omega, God of every beginning and every end, I stand in awe of Your eternal nature. You have set the universe in motion and hold all of time in Your hands. Guide me through the moments of my life; let me see every beginning and ending through Your eternal lens. Grant me the wisdom to cherish every moment, knowing that in every tick of the clock, You are present, leading me from beginning to end. Amen.

Today as you stand on the timeline of your life, remember that the Alpha and Omega walks with you. From every sunrise to every sunset, His eternal presence is a promise, guiding you from the beginning of your story to its glorious end.

ACTION STEPS:

1. Surrender your worries to God.
2. Pray for faith and patience when faced with uncertainty or difficulty.
3. Trust in God's promises for your future.

IMPORTANT TAKEAWAYS:

- All beginnings are rooted in God (alpha), and all endings lead back to Him (omega). Remembering this helps us see our lives from an eternal perspective—everything starts from Him; everything leads back to Him.
- Trust in God's sovereignty. He has complete control over every situation in your life.
- Find hope in transitions. In every ending lies a new beginning; trust God to guide you through these transitions.

APPENDIX

RECEIVING SALVATION

For God so loved the world that he gave his one and only Son, that whoever believes in him shall not perish but have eternal life.

—John 3:16 (NIV)

If you wish to receive the free gift of Salvation through Jesus Christ, pray:

Dear heavenly Father,

I come before You today, acknowledging that I am a sinner. I have done things that are not pleasing to You, and I have lived my life apart from you. But I believe in your great love for me as shown through Your Son Jesus Christ.

I believe that Jesus is Your Son, that He came to earth, lived a perfect life, died on the cross for my sins, and rose again to give me new life. I believe in the promise of John 3:16 that because of Jesus, I can have eternal life.

Today, I turn away from my sinful ways, and I put my trust in Jesus. I accept Him as my Lord and Savior. I ask for Your forgiveness, and I choose to follow You from this day forward.

Thank You for Your love, Your mercy, and Your grace. Thank You for the gift of eternal life through Jesus Christ.

In Jesus's name, I pray. Amen.

Welcome to a Journey of Faith

Congratulations on taking the first steps on your journey of faith. Whether you've recently made a commitment to follow Jesus Christ or are exploring what it means to have a relationship with Him, you are embarking on a transformative adventure. Faith is not just a one-time decision but a continuous journey of growth, discovery, and deepening relationship with God.

Christianity is centered on the life, death, and resurrection of Jesus Christ. Christians believe that Jesus is the Son of God, fully divine and fully human, and that through His sacrifice on the cross, He has made a way for us to be reconciled with God. By accepting Jesus as our Lord and Savior, we receive forgiveness for our sins and the gift of eternal life.

As a new believer, you may have many questions and a desire to understand more about your faith. The Bible is the foundational text for Christians, and it is a rich resource for learning about God, His character, and His plan for humanity. You are encouraged to read it regularly, starting perhaps with the Gospels (Matthew, Mark, Luke, and John), which tell the story of Jesus's life.

Prayer is another vital aspect of the Christian life. It is a way of communicating with God, expressing our thanks, seeking His guidance, and bringing our needs before Him. Don't worry if you're unsure how to pray—speak from your heart. God values sincerity and openness.

Being part of a community of believers is also crucial. Seek out a local church where you can learn, grow, and serve alongside others. The Christian life is not meant to be lived in isolation, and the support and fellowship of a community can be a great source of strength.

Remember that growth in faith is a process, and there may be ups and downs along the way. Don't be discouraged by challenges or questions; they are a normal part of the journey. Seek guidance from mature Christians, and be assured that God is with you every step of the way.

Welcome to the family of God! May your faith journey be filled with joy, discovery, and a deepening sense of God's love for you.

NOTES

Day	Scriptures
1	Genesis 1:1, 1:2, 1:31; Proverbs 3:5
2	Exodus 3:14; Psalm 56:3; Hebrews 13:8; Revelation 1:8
3	Genesis 17:1; Psalm 91:1
4	Psalm 8:1; Luke 22:42; Proverbs 18:10
5	Genesis 2:4; Romans 5:8; James 4:8; Philippians 4:6–7
6	Genesis 22:14; Philippians 4:19; 2 Corinthians 9:8
7	Exodus 15:26; James 5:15; Isaiah 55:9; Psalm 147:3
8	Exodus 14:14; Psalm 20:1–5; Exodus 17:15
9	Deuteronomy 33:29; Psalm 46:1; Ephesians 6:10–18:2; Samuel 22:31; Hebrews 13:5
10	2 Corinthians 5:21; Ephesians 2:8–9; Jeremiah 23:6
11	1 Samuel 17:45; Deuteronomy 31:6; Psalm 46:7
12	Genesis 16:13; 1 Samuel 16:7
13	Matthew 1:23; Psalm 139:7–10, 46:10; John 14:16–17
14	Psalm 23:6; Romans 8:28; Deuteronomy 7:9
15	Romans 8:15; Galatians 3:26
16	1 John 1:9; Ephesians 4:32; Psalm 99:8
17	John 1:29; Luke 12:8; Matthew 16:16
18	John 14:27; Psalm 29:11; 1 Peter 5:7
19	Psalm 31:5, 33:4; 1 John 1:7; John 8:32
20	Leviticus 20:7–8; 1 Thessalonians 5:23; Mathew 11:28–30
21	James 1:17; Revelation 19:11; 2 Peter 1:3; Genesis 21:33
22	Micah 7:18–19; Psalm 59:10, 103:8
23	Psalm 18:2, 62:6–7
24	1 Samuel 2:3; Psalm 139:4; James 4:10; James 1:5; Proverbs 2:6
25	Psalm 19:1, 29:3; Isaiah 6:3; Matthew 5:16

ABOUT THE AUTHOR

James Johannes is a Christian writer and fellow traveler on the faith journey. A layman deeply committed to living out the teachings of Christ in everyday life, his writings are a reflection of a heart earnestly seeking to encourage and uplift fellow disciples as they navigate their own spiritual paths.

With a life richly woven through with personal experiences and lessons learned in the walk with God, James brings a relatable and sincere voice to his readers. He doesn't position himself as an expert theologian or a distant academic but rather as a friend and mentor who shares from his heart with humility and transparency. His writings are born out of a genuine desire to make a difference in the lives of others, offering support, wisdom, and encouragement gleaned from his own journey.

A deep empathy for the Christian life's struggles and triumphs characterizes James's writing approach. He understands that faith is a journey, often filled with questions and challenges, and his work seeks to provide guidance, comfort, and reassurance to those seeking to deepen their relationship with God.

In His Name: A Thirty-Day Journey through the Names of God is a culmination of James's passion for exploring the depths of God's character and sharing those discoveries in a way that is accessible and relevant to believers today. This book is not just a project for him; it's an offering of love to his fellow Christians—a tool to help them grow in their understanding and intimacy with the Lord. It is an invitation from James to you, the reader, to join in this beautiful and ongoing conversation about who God is and how we can live more fully in His presence.

THANK YOU!

Dear Friend,

My heartfelt thanks to you for journeying through the pages of *In His Name: A Thirty-Day Journey through the Names of God.* Your commitment to exploring the divine tapestry of God's names has been both an honor and a joy to witness.

Above all, we give thanks to God, whose names and character have been the foundation of this sacred exploration. May this journey deepen your connection to God the Father, God the Son, and God the Holy Spirit, and enrich your spiritual journey.

With heartfelt gratitude,
James Johannes

Printed in the United States
by Baker & Taylor Publisher Services